UNSCRAMBLING THE
MILLENNIAL
PARADOX

Why the "Unreachables" May Be Key
to the Next Great Awakening

ALLIE ANDERSON

DEFENDER

CRANE, MO

Unscrambling the Millennial Paradox: Why the "Unreachables" May Be Key to the Next Great Awakening

Defender Publishing
Crane, MO 65633
©2019 by Allie Anderson
All rights reserved. Published 2019.
Printed in the United States of America.

ISBN: 978-1-948014-20-5

A CIP catalog record of this book is available from the Library of Congress.

Cover design by Jeffrey Mardis.

All Scripture quotations from the King James Version.

This book is dedicated to both the servant and the seeker: to the faithful who have worked to reach a lost generation, and to those whose search has led them away from the church. May you find each other and make a meaningful connection that lasts a lifetime within the Body of Christ.

To God, may all of my endeavors be always as unto you.

To John and Kat, my Millennial and Post-Millennial children, who make me proud every single day. May you follow the Lord always.

To Randy and his bunch, my love always.

Contents

INTRODUCTION

FEW, IF ANY, WOULD ARGUE when I say that the Millennial generation may be the most notorious the world has ever seen. Certainly, never has a single age group been given so many negative labels and stereotypes. Beyond this, the consensus is correspondingly polarized: It seems that any given member of the public, asked for an opinion about this generation, has an equal probability of answering with sentiments of love or hate.

How, then, has the world produced this segment of the population that draws such animated, emotionally charged reactions from older generations? Moreover, it is doubtful that many of those critiquing our youth are aware of the torrent of personal crises wreaking havoc upon this crowd—epidemics such as depression, anxiety, suicide, alcoholism, and drug addiction, all of which claim more lives from this demographic each year.

As an increasing number of stories in the media report that Millennials are leaving the church *en masse* to search for answers to life's questions elsewhere, the challenge Christians face today then becomes: How can this destruction of our youth be halted and reversed? Can we turn this momentum around to reach these lost souls for Christ? A close look at these and similar issues make up the pages of this book.

A disclaimer: It isn't my intention to victimize or villainize either the old or the young; rather, my effort is to analytically and compassionately point out difficulties faced by *all currently cohabitating* generations to foster a setting where common ground can be found and where previously burned bridges can be rebuilt.

First, a look at some key terms. The birth years of members of various generations have been defined differently by several organizations. For clarity and simplicity, we will observe the following as defined by the Pew Research Center:[1]

Silent Generation: 1928–1945
Baby Boomers: 1946–1964
Generation X: 1965–1980
Millennials: 1981–1996
Post-Millennials: 1997–present

Additionally, since many issues that Millennials and Post-Millennials face are intertwined, and stereotypes often apply to members of each of these groups, I won't use the prefix "post"; I'll refer to all of those born from 1981 to the present as Millennials, unless specified otherwise.

This book is intended to function as an exposé of the direction in which the world is heading and how our youth are being misled into perpetuating this destruction. Through this work, the SkyWatch team sends a charge to the members of the modern church—young and old— to leave behind their comfort zones, to break barriers, to drop stereotypes and generational labels, to try to understand and reach each other, and to bring the Bride of Christ back together as a unified Body. The Church, this country, and even the world itself are at a pivotal moment that will never come again; every day brings additional destruction upon the lost and dying youth around us. Will you dare to turn the page, engage in this book, and become a part of the solution to the problem?

THE TERMINAL
GENERATION

DID YOU KNOW that suicide is now the second-highest killer of young adults between the ages of fifteen to twenty-four years, and that this same destroyer is on the rise among individuals under age fourteen? In fact, the Centers for Disease Control and Prevention (CDC) asserts that nearly 160,000 youths ages ten through twenty-four are hospitalized each year for self-inflicted wounds.[2] If this surprises you, you may likewise be unaware that the CDC, in its mortality report for 2016, stated that nearly sixty-four thousand people between the ages of fifteen and thirty-five died of drug overdoses during that year alone.[3] As if this were not enough to raise concern, a recent spike in cirrhosis of the liver—linked specifically to alcohol abuse—has replaced HIV as the sixth-leading cause of death in people ages twenty-five to forty-four. This may make more sense when it is discovered that nearly three-quarters of members of the Millennial generation report dealing with depression levels high enough to impede job performance in the professional setting,[4] and that anxiety for our youth is at an all-time high.

Simultaneously, the Public Religion Research Institute recently released statistics stating that "the number of Americans ages 18–29 who have no religious affiliation has nearly quadrupled in the last 30 years."[5] Looking around at modern society, we may not find this surprising. However, trends show that our youth are not *all* abandoning spirituality—as the number of individuals claiming atheism is likewise on the decline[6]—but many are merely departing from *Christianity* and *the Church*. Many of these instead opt for nontraditional affiliations, such as online witchcraft covens,[7] while Islam has accelerated to become the fastest-growing religion in the world.[8]

What is causing this exodus of our young people from Christianity? Many are quick to point out that the Church of today indeed has a problem, but when it's time to propose answers to the dilemma, far fewer individuals are ready to speak out. For those who venture to answer such looming questions, the responses often land within the realm of church makeovers or even Millennial-bashing. Many religious institutions have attempted to retain their young audiences by resorting to visible upgrades to please a quickly diminishing crowd with such amenities as overhauled facilities, modernized worship services, and even on-site coffee shops. However, in light of the continually climbing numbers of those who are departing from our churches, it seems that a deeper issue is on the rise—one with eternally dire consequences. Sadly, while churches fumble frantically for solutions, the devastating and even terminal epidemics such as those mentioned previously sweeping over our nation's youth continue to gain momentum.

MILLENNIALS: THE MOST "PICKED ON" GENERATION?

It is no question that the Millennials have taken more heat for what the older generation considers to be their "antics" than any other addressed by today's media. Certainly, the age gap between younger and older adults is affected by issues such as technology, identity politics (more on this later), economics, and others. To claim there is a generation gap is a vast understatement. As tension between our older and younger age groups continues to mount, the latter increasingly turns to solutions such as alcohol, witchcraft, and drugs, etc., in a desperate search for what they have not found in religion. In the meantime, a societal shift has contributed to the largest age-related gap the world has ever seen, and our young population has been labeled with such names as the "Unreachable Generation"[9] and the "Worst Generation."[10] Sadly, members of these age brackets are on record as the most fatherless populace—as well as the most isolated and lonely. How does this notorious collective—one of the largest the world has ever seen—find itself cut off from (and even *resented* by) older generations, seeking satisfaction they seemingly cannot find and turning to such self-destructive measures as they go about their quest? What is it that they are searching *for*, and precisely *why* is there so much friction between age bands? Surely the abrasion that creates this divide is much more acute than typical generation gaps, yet to label it as such is the closest many have come to pinpointing a real culprit. The question then becomes: What is *really* at the heart of the matter with our young people of today? Many offer quick answers to this query, presuming that a surface-level answer has the depth necessary to encapsulate all the complicated issues at the core of such a question. Sadly, as we spend our time deliberating—even debating—possible causes and solutions for the desperate situation our youth are in, for many, the clock is rapidly running out.

SUICIDE, DRUG ABUSE, AND ALCOHOL ABUSE

In 2017, the CDC reported that the rate of suicide among teens and young adults has nearly tripled since 1940[11] and suicide is now "the third-leading cause of death for youth between the ages of 10 and 24.[12] In a separate report, the CDC named suicide as the "second-leading cause of death among people ages 15 to 24, increasing by 7% in this group each year between 2014 and 2016."[13] The rate drops, once again, to become the third-leading cause of death when the age bracket is widened to include all individuals between ages twenty-five and forty-four.[14] An additionally alarming discovery is that "suicide rates even rose among children ages 1 to 14, increasing around 9% each year during the study period."[15]

Taking these reports together, there is an overlap that may seem a little confusing, so I will clarify: When we arrive at the figure that applies to those between the ages of ten to twenty-four years, suicide is the *third*-leading cause of death. Once that window narrows and we look at individuals *only between the ages of fifteen and twenty-four* years, that percentage climbs to make suicide the *second*-leading cause of death. By the time we pass the twenty-four-year-old mark, the rate returns to *third* place. The spike we see in the numbers related to teenage girls between the ages of fifteen and twenty-four is backed by additional statistics: Between the years of 2010 and 2016, "suicide rates among young and teenage girls rose by 70%…according to CDC data."[16]

With suicide rates escalating to these levels, the CDC estimates successful attempts at self-harm to be responsible for approximately 4,600 lives lost by people between the ages of ten and twenty-four each year.[17] While this is a devastating number, it only accounts for those who *died* as a result of their actions. This number doesn't factor in the countless unsuccessful suicide attempts each year. As mentioned earlier, approximately 157,000 individuals between the ages of ten and twenty-four are treated in emergency rooms throughout America for self-inflicted injuries each year. Beyond this, there is no way to count how many attempt suicide but are not hospitalized—either because they are too ashamed to seek treatment or because their injuries are minimal.

Furthermore, "a nationwide survey of high school students in the United States found that 16% of students reported seriously considering suicide, 13% reported creating a plan, and 8% reported trying to take their own life in the 12 months preceding the survey."[18]

In addition, the CDC's National Center for Health Statistics (NCHS) recently released its annual comprehensive health and mortality report, which indicates the first drop in life expectancy the US has seen since 1993. Surprisingly, the culprits are stated to be drug abuse, alcohol abuse resulting in liver disease, and suicide. "Death rates for Americans ages 15 to 44 rose by around 5% each year between 2013 and 2016, and drugs, alcohol and suicide are chiefly to blame, the CDC report says."[19] Drug overdoses claimed the lives of 63,600 people, with men between twenty-four and thirty-five experiencing overdose rates that increased by 25 percent each year between 2014 and 2016, while women ages fifteen to twenty-four saw a 19 percent increase. These numbers seem conservative compared to a report released in August 2018 by the National Institute on Drug Abuse, which states that more than 72,000 deaths due to drug overdose occurred in 2017 (this report, however, did not itemize by age group).[20]

Beyond the issue of drug abuse and overdose, alcohol abuse spiked, with liver disease replacing HIV as the "sixth-leading killer of adults ages 25 to 44 in 2016," while men and women between the ages of twenty-five and thirty-four saw an increase in deaths as a result of liver disease and cirrhosis, escalating between 8 percent and 11 percent per year between 2006 and 2016.[21] The increase in deaths related to the end stages of liver damage between 1999 and 2016 was 65 percent, with alcohol consumption stated as the major cause.

Liver disease (cirrhosis), which previously primarily plagued older generations, has seen a conversion in the age of its victims; the largest affected group is now adults ages twenty-five to thirty-four. Liver specialist Elliot B Tapper, MD, of the Institute for Healthcare Policy and Innovation for the University of Michigan, noticed this change in the affected age range as a "disturbing shift in demographics among the patients with liver failure."[22] Tapper, with the help of comrade Neehar Parikh, MD, MS, "confirms that in communities across the country more young people are drinking themselves to death,"[23] and notes that those in the age group of twenty-five to thirty-four are currently experiencing the fastest average increase in cirrhosis deaths, which are up nearly 11 percent each year.[24] While cirrhosis of the liver can be caused by viruses such as hepatitis C or conditions such as fatty liver disease, these doctors state the majority of cases among those age twenty-five to thirty-four, sadly, are preventable because they are brought on by alcohol abuse.

ANXIETY AND DEPRESSION

The fact that drug overdose, alcohol abuse, and suicide rates have skyrocketed could be a byproduct of the fact that many recent studies link Millennials to higher rates of and risk for having mental health issues such as depression, anxiety, and thoughts of suicide than were evident in previous generations. In fact, recall this aforementioned statistic: As many as 70 percent of Millennials reported suffering depression severe enough to interfere with their job performance.[25]

The American Psychiatric Association (APA) recently revealed that Millennials in the age bracket of twenty to thirty-seven are the most anxious generation.[26] In fact, according to the APA, "12% of millennials have an officially diagnosed anxiety disorder—nearly double the percentage of baby boomers. Other studies have found that 30 percent of working millennials are classified with general anxiety, and a 2014 American College Health Association (ACHA) assessment found that 61 percent of college students experience frequent anxiety."[27]

Some may argue that one contributor to the increase is the correlating rise in awareness of and openness regarding such issues. While this could certainly account for some of the surge, epidemics such as those previously mentioned—alcohol abuse, drug abuse, religion-seeking, and rising suicide rates—cannot be ignored. Credibility is added when these heightened percentages are considered in conjunction with the self-destructive tendencies embraced by the youngest generations.

Possible causes of the soaring numbers of those who suffer from depression, anxiety, and thoughts of suicide are numerous and will be addressed throughout this book. For this moment, suffice it to say our younger generations are grappling in a mental battle that for many, obviously, feels like a losing game.

SINGLE-PARENT EPIDEMIC

A Pew Research Center Report recently stated that Millennials are now the largest age group within the demographic of single-mother homes, accounting for roughly four million US households with children under eighteen years of age.[28] Additionally, these account for half of the 8.3 million American households with a single parent, while the number of homes occupied by married couples declined from 45 to 37 percent.[29] Children of divorced and single parents face higher odds of having many complications, such as the risk of abuse and neglect, behavioral and emotional problems, educational challenges, criminal activity, drug and alcohol abuse, suicidal thoughts, promiscuity, teen parenthood, and dropping out of school, and a smaller percentage of these individuals claim having a religious faith than their age-mates from intact families.[30] While every single parent should be supported and congratulated for the brave decision to choose life, the road ahead for both parent and child is a tough one, often yielding many other types of pain and difficulties.

WITCHCRAFT AT ALL-TIME HIGH

Even as I write this, the news is filled with stories of Millennials who have ditched Christian churches to take up witchcraft. The *New York Times*, on November 20, 2018, released a story that stated, "from crystal subscription boxes to astrologist-created lip balm, the metaphysical has gone mainstream."[31] The story asserts that the number of Americans who identify as Wiccan or pagan is up from 700,000 (which was the number ten years ago), to 1.5 million today—more than doubled! Likewise, "Stella Bugbee, editor-and-chief and president of the Cut, told the Atlantic that horoscope content traffic increased 150% from 2016 to 2017."[32] These individuals proudly network over social media websites, which have enabled them to join forces across great distances.

Consider, for example, the "digital covens" now turning up on the Internet. An organization of African-American witches held their third-annual Black Witch Convention in October 2018, where "hundreds of young black women…are leaving Christianity in favor of their ancestors' African spiritual traditions and [found] a sense of power in the process."[33] Over the last ten years, witchcraft has grown in popularity amongst Millennials, and digital covens have made it easier for these individuals to network—not to mention that they have made the practice of witchcraft more accessible from the privacy of one's home. For those who may have shied away from such activity previously due to the stigma attached, this is no longer an issue, thanks to technology that grants anonymity through avatars, pseudo names or "handles," and access to the affiliation without attending public meetings. A Boston University professor, Margarita Guillory, said: "The internet is almost becoming like a hush harbor for these witches"[34] who practice activities such as "[building] altars to ancestors so they can seek their advice on everything from romance to professional advancement, cast spells using emoji to help banish depression, surround themselves with crystals in the hope that they will relieve stress, and burn Sage to cleanse their apartments of negative energy."[35] Because of the anonymity allowed in these digital covens, entries are anonymous and privacy is protected. Some participants previously attended Bible-believing churches, but many left for reasons similar to those that we will discuss later at length.

MILLENNIALS LEAVING THE CHURCH

Sadly, Millennials are leaving the church in flocks. A nation once primarily populated with churchgoing, Bible-believing Christians has become a society where regular attendance is hardly prioritized anymore. In fact, within our under-thirty population, only two out of ten report believing attending church is important or even worthwhile.[36] While more than half of the Millennials raised in church have stopped showing up on Sunday mornings, 35 percent have a strong aversion to it, stating that the religious institution actually "does more harm than good."[37]

Considering all the information presented so far in this chapter, it's obvious to Bible-believing Christians that we have a society of youths who desperately need God. I would even venture to say that what they're really searching for is *Him* when they engage in many destructive activities. Yet, ironically, in the US—where Christianity, church, and myriad other forms of religious activity are easily available—we see them walking away and seeking answers to life's problems elsewhere. The question that ensues then becomes the heart of this book:

Why is our youth leaving Christianity, and what can we do to reverse this trend?

A FRUSTRATED OLDER GENERATION

Many members of previous generations find it difficult to understand the epidemics plaguing today's young people. They also have a hard time understanding how young people living in such a blessed nation could turn away from God and leave His church. Considering the problematic issues that have been pointed out, alongside the younger generation's abandonment of Christianity, many older folks reminisce about the hardships that they faced in *their* early adulthood, citing their faith in God as being the *very thing that kept them from succumbing to such troubles*. It's not at all uncommon for an older person to note the statistics mentioned at the beginning of this chapter while reflecting upon all of the resources available to our youth, and noting today's situation in contrast to their own with frustration, bewilderment, and even indignation. Statements such as, "If I had had the opportunities that our youth of today enjoy when I was that age, I would never… [insert negative Millennial behavior here]." One of the most stupefying realities for many to grasp about young adults today is the fact that they have so many assets that were either unavailable or—at the very least— much scarcer to previous generations. Many look upon the youth of today with envy that quickly morphs into resentment over "wasted" or "underappreciated" resources. When these same critics add to this the fact that the young members of our society struggle with depression, addiction, disenchantment, and aversion to the church, they often conclude that Millennials are wasteful, spoiled, entitled, and ungrateful.

"IF ONLY I'D HAD WHAT YOU HAVE…"

When I observe the way some members of our older generation often view the young people of today, I recall a scene in *Castaway*[38] starring Tom Hanks. In this movie, Hanks' character, Chuck Noland, survives a plane crash and is marooned on a deserted island, where he is forced to survive alone. His only resources are the work of his hands and scarce material goods that washed ashore amongst the debris from the plane crash. A highlight of the film is when, after hours of frustratingly fruitless attempts involving dried plant matter and two sticks, the stranded Chuck *finally* succeeds in starting a fire. Viewers celebrate this accomplishment alongside the main character as he triumphantly basks in the warmth and glow of his hard-earned flames.

When, at last, Hanks' character is rescued four years later, a huge reception is hosted in his honor: a "welcome back" party featuring ironies such as a buffet of plentiful seafood and a friend inviting him to go fishing (as though he hadn't seen enough seafood and fishing over the past four years). When the crowd leaves after the banquet, Chuck stares at the remnants of the feast, slowly turning over a crab leg in his hands and then setting it down again with repulsion. He picks up a long-stemmed lighter (the type used to light a propane barbecue grill; in this scene, presumably used to light the sterno canisters warming the food), and looks at it thoughtfully. He repeatedly pulls the "trigger" on the tool, causing the flame to ignite, then go out, ignite again, and go out again. It's a brief scene and no words are spoken, but we can easily read the look on Chuck Noland's face: *If only I had one of these back on that island, life would have been so much easier!*

Often, I see a similar response from older individuals who note the resources available to younger generations today. Few would debate that, considering available amenities, our young people, in many ways, make up one of the wealthiest, if not the wealthiest, generations in history. Statistics still report high poverty levels throughout the world and even in the US (12.3 percent in the US as of the end of 2017[39]), but our *definition* of poverty has likewise changed over the years. Many who are *justly* categorized as being impoverished today still have access to many resources unavailable to generations past. We now define poverty at a variety of levels gauging differing qualities of life: income poverty, relative poverty, extreme poverty, and absolute poverty,[40] to name a few. Absolute poverty is defined by the United Nations Educational, Scientific and Cultural Organization as measuring "poverty in relation to the amount of money necessary to meet basic needs such as food, clothing, and shelter."[41] When older folks recall struggles of their youth, they're usually speaking of *absolute poverty.*

I'm in no way saying this isn't an issue in our modern world. My point, rather, is that even by today's standards, many times, members of an older generation see a level of wealth that wasn't available to them when they were at the correlating age. For example, a large percentage of our youth of today is provided with an education that, in most school districts, begins at preschool and extends through the twelfth grade. This is in huge contrast to those who are, for example, in their nineties, and whose education (if any) probably began in middle childhood and likely was cut short when they needed to work to help the family's income (in contrast to today's education, which is mandated until the late teens).

Using education as an example, a young person may complain to an older one about the school workload or about the educational experience being tedious or even *boring*. In such a case, the older person might adopt a facial expression similar to that of Chuck Noland in *Castaway* as he stared into the previously unavailable convenience of fire on demand. At this moment, Millennials likely have no idea that their comments seem offensive, while older adults likewise can't fathom *how* the students are unaware that their attitude seems ungrateful. Worse, when youth declare that the school experience is causing such anxiety that they are compelled to turn to bad behavior or substance abuse as a means of coping, they receive harsh judgment by those who were forced as youths to "find a way to make ends meet" without having such advantages. Much intergenerational tension centers on just such circumstances and indignation, but many issues are less obvious, hidden in nuance, and will thus be exposed within the pages of this book.

On the other hand (using the example in the previous paragraph as a template for how such issues come to a boiling point), youths who have complained (and are likewise unaware of the offense their words have caused) are understandably off-put by the harshness of older people, whose comments seem as though they come out of left field. It's likely that parents or guardians of Millennials (understandably) have let their children know that going to school is the *only* life option available. This causes youths to feel "trapped" by this educational advantage, despite its unavailability to previous generations. Additionally, romanticized images of "years gone by" portrayed through movies, books, other media, and even older folks' revelries cause young people to perceive life as having been easier in "the old days," and to think that there is no way an older person could *possibly* understand the plight of the young.

At this point, you may be thinking, "You're not telling me anything I don't already know. All you're describing is a typical generation gap."

The *Cambridge Dictionary* defines "generation gap" as "a lack of understanding between older and younger people that results from different experiences of life."[42] If only the issues faced by today's society members were that simple.

Unfortunately, the rift between the current age factions is much larger than in any previous generation. While many problems *do* stem from this, the essence of the divide is much greater than a mere separation of years. In fact, the world has never seen an intergenerational chasm such as the one that exists today. Why is this? Because the world has never seen a generation like this one and has never known financial, economic, and technical/digital influences like those bombarding today's population. Worldwide media, social media, digital interface, multicultural and multireligious blending, political tensions, the breakdown of the family, constant availability of instant gratification, isolation of individuals, and even economic stressors have cultivated a melting pot resulting in the most exceptional generation that the world has ever seen, under the most matchless national setting that has ever existed. Because of this, parents, grandparents, coaches, teachers, ministers, and even employers often are not certain of the most effective way to deal with the young people of today. History certainly offers no template guided by previous experience—successful or otherwise. This inability to relate puts individuals on guard, further dividing age groups.

Worse than, but similar to, this divide is the breach that has formed between our younger population and the church. The same issues that separate generations in the secular world have become, at times, even more severely polarized within the church. As Millennials leave religious institutions in masses to search for fulfillment in false religion, self-seeking pursuits, substance abuse, political trends, or other causes, churches across our nation scramble to find and offer remedies. This lies at the heart of the transformation of many well-meaning churches, whose responses (as referenced briefly at the beginning of this chapter) have included such solutions as offering coffee shops on their campuses, hiring young-looking pastors who sport personal and wardrobe styles previously not permitted within leadership (earrings on men, skinny jeans, etc.), featuring worship services that use contemporary music rather than time-honored hymns, providing more flexible service schedules, posting online streaming and video blogs, conducting social media outreaches, and including additional programs such as intimately small groups that meet between regularly scheduled church services, and much more.

While these things aren't necessarily wrong, many agree that when it comes to barricading the stampede of the Millennials' exodus, these strategies aren't *necessarily working*, either. How does a church adapt to the needs of a contemporary generation? Statistics cited at the beginning of this chapter indicate that these people need God, but sadly, as they abandon their churches (and heartbreakingly, as they also turn away from the gospel of Jesus Christ), their search takes them into a lost and dying world where false religion, sexual immorality, and substance abuse will never fill the void they're trying to fill.

As religious institutions lose the attendance of younger generations by the multitudes, it is essential that we answer the question of what this generation *needs* so that we can intervene before any more souls—or *lives*, for that matter—are lost. It is time for churches to adapt to meet a young populace in a place where they can hear our message without our having to compromise scriptural truth. But this is more easily said than done. To effectively *intervene*, we must properly *diagnose* the core problem. Although many young people may claim that churches are archaic and patriarchal, is that really the heart of their complaint? Or is the problem more ambiguous? Many who speak out claim the issue is deeper, but their reasons seem to contradict each other, leading us to suspect that the youth of today either (1) don't know *what* they want; or (2) are having trouble *articulating* it. Furthermore, quick, surface-level facelifts to make a church appealing to Millennials on a sensory level are generally met with criticism, with young people recoiling from efforts they often deem as fake. What's a church to do? The reasons Millennials often cite for leaving are indeed clues to deeper problems—which are likely issues so difficult to express that they often go unspoken.

The answer is not as simple as the need for churches to "update" to meet the needs of a modern generation. If this were the case, we would have found the solution by now. We've already acknowledged that many churches have made such changes. Yet, despite these efforts, the divide between the mission of Christ and our youth of today widens. Clearly, we've missed something very important. Sadly, as we fumble for solutions, a hurting and lost generation is resorting to increasingly devastating—often, even terminal—remedies for their pain.

> Neither pray I for these alone, but for them also which shall believe on me through their word; That they all may be one; as thou, Father, art in me, and I in thee, that they also may be one in us: that the world may believe that thou hast sent me. And the glory which thou gavest me I have given them; that they may be one, even as we are one: I in them, and thou in me, that they may be made perfect in one; and that the world may know that thou hast sent me, and hast loved them, as thou hast loved me. (John 17:20–23)

Just as God is unified between the Father, the Son, and the Holy Spirit, Jesus prayed that the Church would be unified. We are to be fused with each other so that we can, in turn, be joined with God. As individuals within the Body, members of varying age brackets, and even those throughout our society all seem to be divided in unparalleled ways, the battle before us to reunite and reach a dying generation is increasingly paramount.

REUNITING: IS IT POSSIBLE?

A key to reaching our younger generations is our willingness and ability to understand and relate to them. We must set aside frustration and judgment and display a readiness to discover who they are, find out what they need, figure out what motivates them, and determine *how to reach them*. However, before you assume that this book is intended to victimize our younger generations or presume that I'm suggesting that we haven't invested enough resources in our youth, please understand that is not the direction of this book. In fact, throughout these pages, I will assert that, among other complicated obstacles, what we're facing today is the widest generation gap that history has ever seen, followed by a socioeconomic climate unlike any the world has ever known. Furthermore, events leading up to today have culminated in what could be described as a cruel generational experiment with our youth as its subjects, and it's up to all of us to map out a path through this chasm before the future is forever pivoted by its current turning point. If our young population continues in this self-destructive direction, their descendants will suffer the same confusion and pain. The time is now to intervene for *all subsequent generations*, or we could lose our opportunity.

The Road Trip to Virginia

Recently, several members of the staff of Defender Publishing/Skywatch TV—Tom Horn, Joe Horn, Donna Howell, and myself—took a business trip to Virginia. This involved a long drive (about a day and a half in each direction) and three overnight hotel stays. On the first day, after we had made the first leg of the journey and settled into our lodging, we went to a local restaurant to have dinner. As we ate, our conversation meandered in an informal tone, until abruptly Tom Horn shifted the topic.

"Allie, did you read the articles I linked to you in an email yesterday?"

I recalled the email, but had been so busy getting ready for our trip that I hadn't read the stories yet. I told him that I intended to read them once we returned home.

"They explain that suicide rates, drug use and overdose, alcohol abuse, depression, anxiety, child abuse, and many other destructive behavioral epidemics are sweeping through our younger generations," he said. "Furthermore, Millennials are leaving the church by the scores."

He shifted his weight in his chair and stared into the distance reflectively for a moment. "Now, I'm a member of the Baby Boomers, and I know that a lot of people in my generation are frustrated with the Millennials right now. But I see a lot of really good qualities within them as well, and I don't understand why they're so off-track. It really bothers me to think that an entire generation of people are losing their way and falling away from God, and I want to know what can be done about it."

Some discussion then took place among the four of us, each of us suggesting theories and bringing up discussion points. We exchanged ideas about the generation gap—especially as it stands in many churches—along with our thoughts about the influence of technology, indoctrination within schools, and even consequences of identity politics (again, more on this term later) upon our youth. A little deeper into the conversation, Tom said something I'll never forget:

"I know I don't understand everything about our younger population, but I *just cannot turn my back* and watch an entire generation of people Christ died for become lost for all eternity. I *have to* do everything I can to intervene."

This statement was followed by a moment of silence. I stirred my iced tea thoughtfully while the others at the table pondered quietly as well. After a moment, Tom spoke again.

"Do you remember the movie, *The Cross and the Switchblade?*"

Of course I did. When I was very little (probably three years old), a youth rally had taken place in a community center in my earliest hometown of Amity, Oregon. A huge gymnasium had been rented for the event, which was hosted with an open invitation to everyone in the area, free of cost. During the gathering, lights in the gym were kept very low and a giant projector screen, visible from all angles from the bleachers in the gymnasium, displayed the movie in its entirety. (*The Cross and the Switchblade* is the screenplay adaptation of a nonfiction book of the same name written by David Wilkerson. The work tells the story of Wilkerson's journey from being a small-town preacher in Pennsylvania to fulfilling his calling to minister to street gangs in downtown New York. The story highlights Wilkerson's encounter with notorious gang member Nicky Cruz, and Cruz's subsequent conversion to Christ. The chain of events portrayed in both the book and the movie prompted Wilkerson's founding of the well-known national ministry Teen Challenge.)

At the end of the evening following the showing of the movie, an altar call was held, and many in attendance were brought to the Lord. Although the memory of that long-ago event has been vivid throughout my entire life, it wasn't until just a few years ago that I learned that it was my own dad who had organized that entire event.

My thoughts returned to the conversation at hand.

"Yes, I remember it well," I answered.

"Do you remember that scene where David Wilkerson was preaching to that New York gang, and he was thinking that no one was listening?" he asked. "He keeps preaching, and suddenly, there's this breakthrough moment in his sermon when one of the gang members looks up and says 'Keep it up, Preach. You're coming through.'"[43]?

I nodded, vaguely recalling that scene.

Tom leaned forward in his seat purposefully, making eye contact with each of us in turn. With his index finger, he tapped on the table as he spoke.

"How do we get to that place with the modern youth?"

Another moment of silence.

Tom continued, "How do we get the message of the gospel of Christ into their hands, in a format they will accept? How do we go from blank stares and generational tension to a place where a Millennial finally looks us in the eye and says, 'Keep it up, Preach. You're coming through.'?"

For the rest of the meal, Tom, Joe, Donna, and I pursued this topic. After dinner, we continued the conversation at our hotel until late into the night. The next day as we drove, this subject was our focus. I found myself in the backseat taking notes in a frantic effort to preserve every point. In fact, finding an answer to this question dominated the remainder of the trip. By the end of the expedition, the book project I was working on at the time (which is still forthcoming) was placed on a back burner, and the mission of this book escalated to the top of the priority publishing list.

THE CROSS AND THE SWITCHBLADE

The moment in *The Cross and the Switchblade* Tom was referring to plays out a little differently in the book than it did in the movie (some scenes were rearranged for the film adaptation); both scenarios bear mentioning. In the movie, David Wilkerson was attempting to preach on the street to a crowd of rowdy, contemptuous onlookers. As Wilkerson stood prayerfully before beginning to speak to the crowd, one of the gang members jested, "Whatsa matter, Preach, you forget your lines?"[44] Wilkerson began to expound on the love of God and His message of hope, challenging the youth to face their sorrow and emptiness by giving the Lord a chance to heal their broken lives.

Later in the same message, the gang member who had previously been poking fun addressed Wilkerson once again, asking, "What do you want me to do, man?"[45]

"Pray with me," Wilkerson answered. "Pray with me, right now, that the Holy Spirit will come into your heart and make you a new man."[46]

The troubled youth answered, "I ain't ready, man."[47]

As Wilkerson began to walk to the next onlooker, the youth stopped him by grasping the preacher's arm. "Hey, don't let it bug you, the kid said. "You're coming through."[48]

The situation around that *particular* line in the book sheds light on an important element of human desire that holds some pertinence to our study.

Wilkerson's written work describes his being allowed to enter the headquarters of one of the prominent street gangs of New York in the early 1960s. He observed a semiclad girl in her teens, who opened the door to him with one hand while holding a beer in her other; she skillfully balanced a cigarette between her lips as she spoke. She then led Wilkerson into a room filled with physically entangled couples who eyed him with disinterest as he walked in. Regarding the message he then attempted to relay, Wilkerson said:

> I didn't try to get a complicated message over to them, just that they were loved. They were loved as they were, there, amid the vodka bottles and the weary, searching sex. God understood what they were looking for when they drank and played with sex, and He yearned for them to have what they were looking

for: stimulation and exhilaration and a sense of being sought after. But not out of a cheap bottle in a cold tenement basement. God had so much higher hopes for them.

Once, when I paused, a boy said, "Keep it up, Preach. You're coming through."[49]

Note the nature of the message Wilkerson was trying to get across: He wasn't attempting to get these misled teens and young adults to wrap their minds around—or even care about, at this point—any complicated theological concept. He was merely trying to meet them *where they were* and let them know that a Higher Power—God—had created them and loved them, *just as they were*, at that very moment. He then told them that God understands the desires and chasing of the human heart, and that the very inner void they were so desperately longing to fill (despite their search in the wrong places) were needs that God *understands and wants to meet.*

In many ways, the problems we're facing with today's youth are entirely different than the issues Wilkerson had to overcome. Some of the problems we stare down today are far more complex than the issues Wilkerson encountered. While the account of Nicky Cruz's conversion and salvation is a miraculous and inspirational show of the triumph of a small-town preacher wielding no weapon other than God's love, it is still a straightforward recounting of a preacher following the calling to an evangelical mission. The issues we meet with our youth, at times, seem much more complicated. Today's young people, in addition to the problems facing previous generations, also have new, intrusive concepts and ideas thrust upon them: advanced technology and social media as a heavy influence, social and economic elements only recently introduced into society, and other factors that have escalated to a point never faced by previous generations. In short, life is so convoluted for our young adults that many of the older populace has dubbed them the "Unreachable Generation."[50] However, our early adults are still human, still made in the image of God, and *still*, deep down, they have the same desires and needs as members of the older crowd. Furthermore, they likewise have an eternal destination that outlasts their time here on earth. We cannot simply turn our backs on them, shrugging them off as "unreachable." There has to be a way to bridge the gap to reach these individuals—no matter how far that distance may seem—and intervene against the crises that are swallowing up our young people.

Despite the differences between Wilkerson's audience and today's, the evangelist's message has a timeless element. While many of our youth may not be found in the headquarters of a notorious gang in downtown New York, their needs and desires are still much as that preacher outlined. And I would wager that the simplest pursuits of human need have been lost amidst the distraction, and our youth have been robbed of the opportunity to understand or articulate *what they're really searching for*.

Applying the simple principles of the all-inclusive search that Wilkerson addressed, I am reminded of the epilogue the Christian band For King and Country added to the cover of their album entitled *Run Wild. Live Free. Love Strong*:

> Run wild. To risk everything. To hold nothing back. To lay it all on the line: your reputation, your success, your comfort. It's that moment when fear is overcome by faith.
>
> Live free. It's not the liberty to do whatever you want whenever and wherever you want, but rather it's living in accordance with the author of humanity and finding freedom by connecting with the Creator who conceived you. Let the light flood into your eyes for the first time, feeling the blood course through your veins, finding the truest version of yourself by knowing the one who knows you even better than you know yourself.
>
> Love Strong. Because you were first loved. Because without love we all perish. Because the earth and the stars can and will pass away, but love; love will always remain.[51]

Wilkerson's message may have been put in simpler words appropriate to the setting he was speaking in, but the message is the same. Every human being is searching for love, acceptance, identity, community, a spiritual connection to a higher power, a sense of accomplishment, and a place to belong. Don't the above words encapsulate what we're all desperately seeking? If the object of our quest is the same for everyone, then why does it seem like our younger generations are so hard to understand?

PARADOXICAL GENERATION

When Tom Horn initially asked how we might get the message of the gospel of Christ into the hands of today's youth, in a format they will accept, our initial responses included digital-based concepts such as phone apps, social media avenues, interactive blogs, and more. (These are all good ideas, and will be discussed later in the book.) However, the conversation quickly changed direction as we concluded that the issue is much deeper than what can be remedied by a digital app. The troubles that contribute to difficulties like the ones addressed at the beginning of this chapter spring from matters of the heart. When we're discussing such devastating difficulties as depression, addiction, and even suicide, the contributing factors obviously run much deeper and are farther-reaching than what a handheld device can cure. Ultimately, such epidemics stem from individuals who struggle with an unsuccessful inward search. The question then becomes, "What are these individuals searching for?"

As mentioned before, there are certain fulfillments all human beings are looking for, but how does that search manifest for different individuals? When factoring in cultural, social, political, economic, and even personal dynamics, how do we help people find solutions and success so they can thrive in a complicated world?

The answer is not found in church facility makeovers or new religious programs. It's discovered by peeling back the layers to reconnect the essence of the human soul to the simplicity of a relationship with God—and His church—in a world that has complicated the human plight nearly beyond recognition.

This is the crux of the church's new mission.

Did We Take a Wrong Turn Somewhere?

Introducing: The Notorious Generation

The young generations of today are possibly the most notorious in history for their "antics." It seems, in fact, that many older folks love to hate these young people, right or wrong. Millennials have taken a regular verbal beating for a variety of attributes they are said to display, and have thus been given many labels, including:

- The Worst Generation[52]
- The Unreachable Generation[53]
- The Me Me Me Generation[54]
- The Most Anxious Generation[55]
- The Most Perfectionist Generation[56]
- The Most Depressed Generation[57]
- The Loneliest Generation[58]

- The Most Isolated Generation[59]
- The Fatherless Generation[60]

Many other labels, whether fair or not, have been placed on our young generations as well. As a group, these people are dubbed with equally harsh and disappointing generalizations. Our youth are accused of being:

- Entitled
- Lazy
- Ambitious
- Narcissistic
- Endowed with an over-inflated sense of self
- Oversensitive
- High-maintenance
- Idealistic
- Unrealistic in their expectations

THE GENERATION ELDERS LOVE TO HATE?

Many older folks love to hate Millennials, but is this fair? After all, the up-and-coming generation shouldn't appear as though it has formed completely out of left field and then surface as adults with attributes that surprise their parents. Many factors contribute to the mental disposition of any generation. Core characteristics are formed over time and are shaped by many influences, including economic status, cultural setting, religious influence, political trends, peer groups, social impacts, media, recent history, and others nearly impossible to quantify. What shapes a society is carved out over a considerable length of time, and many of elements have already built momentum long before the members of a particular age bracket have even been born. So, how did we get to where we are? Often, the philosophical undertone is set gradually, below the radar, while the population quietly—and often unknowingly—acclimates. Unfortunately, seeds are often allowed to germinate over subsequent years, and once the full harvest manifests, the response can be indignation toward the youth who supposedly allowed such changes to take place.

John Wesley, the eighteenth-century cleric, evangelist, and theologian famous for his influence within the early Methodist denomination, said, "What one generation tolerates, the next generation will embrace."[61] For many, this phrase is a reminder never to allow evil to escalate, lest it get out of hand in future generations. However, there is a slightly different way to interpret it.

As the world evolves throughout cultural history, people adapt. As time moves forward and culture shifts beneath pressures and influences of religion, politics, economics, and social issues, a larger societal evolution is taking place: Society, at any one point, has embedded influences that reach farther into the past than any of its citizens; simultaneously, the changes taking place during any period have the potential to extend beyond the lifespan of any members of the current generation as well. In this way, time serves as a constant chain, linking all who exist on this planet at any given moment. Because of this, belief systems, religions, concepts of morality, governmental policies, and even individual attributes such as work ethic become deeply ingrained into the cultural setting long before a person's birth. Examples of these cultural practices are: (1) adapting ancient religions into modern religions; (2) following traditions with roots we're unaware of; or (3) wearing simple things like nonfunctional elements of wardrobe—ones we don't know the origin of.

For this reason, we'll briefly discuss the evolution of human thinking over the past several centuries. Many books have been written on these subjects, so our study here will be vastly truncated.

Understanding how thinking has modified, slowly migrating farther and farther away from biblical truth and into the enlightenment of self will help expose how beliefs and shifts in thought processes that flew below the radar in previous generations can now run rampant in the minds of our youth. In our understanding of this shift in human philosophy, it does us no good to stand back in indignation and ask, "When/how did this happen?" As we all know, hindsight is always 20/20; our speedy study will show us that humanity has been moving this direction for quite some time—certainly longer than the lifespan of any people who are currently alive. This investigation isn't intended to victimize our youth, nor is it meant to villainize our older generation. However, to find common ground on which to constructively disarm friction between age groups, it is helpful to understand how the human rationale has been reshaped through philosophical enlightenment, education, cultural influences, and religious trends, and how these changes have altered our belief in a higher power, our own identity, and the relation between the two.

How Human Thinking Has Evolved

Key elements of philosophical evolution have taken place over the past couple of centuries, many of which have contributed greatly to mankind's increasing distance from biblical faith and belief in God. These movements, as the reader will note, often cause our search to appeal to our own reason by pointing inward, seeking within ourselves rather than looking to Scripture for answers to life's most difficult questions. In addition to this, as the age of scientific discovery has increasingly flourished, the subsequent sense of accomplishment and faith in our ability to explain the previously unexplainable has reinforced aversions to traditional, biblical faith, which are fortified by each of these movements. These movements are summarized next.

THE PREMODERN ERA

The premodern era in Europe is now referred to as the one before the Renaissance. During this period, cultures tended to be homogenized, and each sect primarily followed the religion of its ancestors. Questions regarding such issues as identity or religion were somewhat scarce due to the cooperative, tribal, or village-like way of existence. Even when a bride was given in marriage to a member of another village or tribe, she was expected to assimilate into her new culture.

Douglas Groothuis, PhD, of the University of Oregon and professor of philosophy at Denver Seminary, sums up the premodern circumstance in his book entitled *Truth Decay: Defending Christianity Against the Challenges of Postmodernism*:

> Premodern cultures typically have little or no cultural or religious diversity, minimal or no social change, have not been affected *by secularization and are prescientific. A premodern society is culturally coherent, social roles are prescribed, and there is little exposure to aliens or foreigners who would endanger its way of life.*[62] (emphasis added)

Later in this work, Groothuis describes civilization in the premodern world followed the examples of their elders, utilizing preexisting methods, traditions, career/trade paths, and religious beliefs, largely without question.

THE RENAISSANCE

The Renaissance occurred toward the middle to end of the premodern era. The word "Renaissance" means "rebirth" and signifies a time when people believed they were experiencing a reawakening in many ways: culturally, politically, artistically, religiously, and even personally. During this period, redefinition of all things classical was on the move. Art, literature, and philosophy were questioned and reapproached; new thoughts and ideas were probed and entertained; global exploration increased; and humanism—which introduced the concept that a person was the center of his or her own universe and that personal achievement was the noblest of pursuits—came to the forefront of focus for many who sought deeper understanding of spiritual matters.

The newfound delight that mankind was taking in personal seeking, success, and expression was further justified by the accomplishment of such men as Leonardo Da Vinci, whose work in many fields revolutionized their separate industries; Filippo Brunelleschi, whose engineering and mathematical skills drove his unprecedented architectural accomplishments; Galileo Galilei, whose mathematic and astrological strides drove studies to new, unmatched levels; and even Nicolaus Copernicus, who asserted that it was actually the sun that was at the center of our solar system.[63]

In addition to these budding scientific and industrial advances, "in 1450, the invention of the Gutenberg printing press allowed for improved communication throughout Europe and for ideas to spread more quickly."[64] This facilitated many changes in the world, but of special significance are: "(1) ideas between cultures were then capable of being published and distributed amongst members of other cultures,"[65] and (2) "thinkers began to develop their thinking outside of, and independent from, a biblical framework. The medieval synthesis of Christian and Greek thought had started to unravel."[66] Ideas lingering from early Greek and Roman religious practices were revived and given a modern, fresh presentation, and many were even absorbed into some individuals' concept of Christianity. In response to some of the corruption introduced to the church during this time, many early, influential men within theology—later referred to by many as "church fathers"—began to rise up in protest, thus polarizing the church. Martin Luther, one of the most memorable of these men, is credited with launching the Protestant Reformation, wherein the Catholic church divided.[67]

THE MODERN ERA

During the modern era, division within the church continued to escalate. Christian apologist Groothuis sums up the crux of the religious revolution taking place during this time:

> To speak very generally, many philosophers of this period began questioning not merely certain Roman Catholic doctrines— such as papal authority and indulgences—but Christianity itself and the idea of the divine revelation as a source of authority… [where the goal for many philosophers was to] free humanity from superstition and found a philosophy and civilization on rational inquiry, empirical evidence and scientific discovery… [and whom] desired a rational, scientific worldview over the perceived irrationality and acrimony stemming from religion, and…humanity's emancipation from received dogma and superstition.[68]

For those who didn't remove God completely from their search, the concept of God was rearranged from that of theism, the belief in the existence of a god, to deism, the belief in the existence of a god, but the simultaneous impression that he does not interact with his creation. Thus, many who still believed in God at all began to view Him as cold, uninvolved, and distant.

Many outspoken scholars during this time, however, protested this revolution of thought. They cited the "death of God"[69] (referring to the removal of a higher power from the framework) within matters of religion, philosophy, and morality as the point at which many other things could become unhinged. The concern was this: If our morality, conduct, and philosophy are rooted in religious values, then where will such attributes wander when we remove the element *to which they are grounded*? Even the notorious Friedrich Nietzsche described the removal of a higher power from one's worldview as taking a "sponge to wipe away the entire horizon."[70]

THE POSTMODERN ERA

By the time the postmodern era was dawning, atheism and agnosticism were rampant. Groothuis asserts: "Modernists and postmodernists are united in their philosophical naturalism. They deny the objective existence of God and the supernatural, and take the material universe to be all there is."[71] During this time, relative objectivity had taken a backseat to what many would call rational thinking. It can be difficult to understand exactly what changed between modernism and postmodernism, but again, Groothuis assists us: "Modernism began with the attempt to discern objective reality without recourse to divine revelation or religious tradition, which it dismissed as merely culturally contingent and ultimately superstitious.... Postmodernists affirm relativism even at the level of language itself."[72] He states that "'religious truth is a special kind of truth' that is not 'an eternal and perfect representation of cosmic reality.'"[73] While many present postmodernism as erratically different from modernism, Groothuis accurately describes postmodernism as modernism that has gone to seed.[74] The postmodern worldview considers truth to be an abstract discovery, obtainable only by the one who individually finds it. In this way, we each have the luxury and prerogative to seek our own "truth."

This means that, outside of the natural realm, truth is anything we *feel* it should be. The search for spiritual or physical guidance or boundaries shifted from that of one based upon moral convictions or belief in a higher power to that of a search indulged through the emotional response of an individual. The revolution that began by questioning the concept of scriptural authority—whether there is a God, and where the lines of morality should thus be drawn—slowly transferred from the societal worldview as it was handed down to children (premodern era) to leaving individuals with *carte blanche* for whether they wanted to believe there is a God at all. If there is no God, there is no standard by which morality is required to be measured. And if morality is left completely up to individual preferences, then we can decide that acts previously considered sinful or even heinous are no longer immoral based upon personal enjoyment. Some individuals even escalated this philosophy by believing that God is a mere state of mind or other attribute found in each of us. Beyond this, people then were given a path by which they could literally choose their own reality, free of judgment from others.

As the seeds of postmodernist worldview germinate, weeds are sown throughout society's garden of truth. The discrepancies that are so often misleading within the search for truth outside the natural realm slowly bleed into the natural realm as well. This, among other elements, has paved the way for the identity politics that our current youth must reconcile themselves to.

In the midst of the chaos that has ensued as a result of truth being "up for grabs," redefinable by anyone who feels the urge at any time they want, individuals with religious beliefs are left scrambling—often to do damage control. The wreckage has at times polarized churches between two positions: 1) acceptance and love to the point of fear-driven complacency, and 2) escalated levels of legalism, backed by threats of hellfire or quippy phrases such as "get right, or get left."

SECULARIZATION, PLURALIZATION, AND PRIVATIZATION

Secularization, pluralization, and privatization have had an enormous impact on the modern generation's thought processes. It seems possible to compartmentalize each of these—and by doing so, limit their influence—but each has a nearly untraceable way of "bleeding out" into surrounding components. The effects can be seen everywhere in small ways, but not always in any one large, readily visible element. Thus, even those who don't necessarily agree with the philosophies behind each of these elements will still be impacted by their vast sway.

Christian anthropologist, speaker, and author Ravi Zacharias is an outspoken advocate for biblical truth in our postmodern times. His teachings are grounded in Scripture, are well thought out, and are argued with compassion toward the nonbeliever—as well as are posed from an individual who has lived his entire life under the minority status of being an American/Canadian who was born in India. At the University of California, Los Angeles, as a guest speaking for the Veritas Forum, Zacharias commented about the impact of secularization, pluralization, and privatization on our modern society.

SECULARIZATION

Secularism as defined by the *Merriam-Webster Dictionary* is the "indifference to or rejection or exclusion of religion and religious considerations."[75] Secularization is, according to Zacharias, "the process by which religious ideas, institutions, and interpretations have lost their social significance."[76] He explains that during the 1960s, against the backdrop of the Vietnam War and political arguments regarding such matters as the sanctity of life beginning to take center stage within the political climate, the traditional religious convictions and values were rapidly losing their social significance. Since then, this shift in values has continued to move in the direction that it was pivoted toward during this time. As a result, religious ideas, institutions, and interpretations have continued to lose their place within our social construct, until the *running truth about absolute truth is that there is no absolute truth*—that is, except for the fact that it is considered an *absolute truth* to say that *there is no absolute truth*. (Confused? Have we twisted the word "truth" enough yet? Apparently not...) This is the type of logic that our youth must attempt to decipher.

In addition to this revolution, Zacharias says:

> The problem...is not with secularization, per say, because ultimately we really don't want a theocracy; we don't want a religious authority ruling the country. History is replete with pathetic examples of what happened when power was arrogated to those who, instead of *representing* God, started to *play* God. But if secularization comes to mean the eviction of the sacred in the public square, where it's not given a free chance at its discourse, that's when you run into the big problem.... When Secularism...has evicted everything that is sacred and made a free-for-all grab for sensation and feeling alone. It will ultimately eradicate a sense of shame [conviction] within a culture, [and] shame is a desperately needed sensation.[77]

Zacharias goes on to explain that shame is essential, as an innate part of our conscience to keep us on the right track and to hold our moral boundaries where God designed. In fact, he describes a nation without shame as a monstrosity in the making.

PLURALIZATION

Pluralism is defined as (among other things) "a state of society in which members of diverse ethnic, racial, religious, or social groups maintain and develop their traditional culture or special interest within the confines of a common civilization."[78] Allow me to preface this part of our study by ensuring the reader that I am in no way saying that the multiethnic status of our great nation is a bad thing. In fact, the plurality of our country is part of what makes it such a strong and thriving force. We are privileged to share in all the wonderful benefits that come with a plurally established culture. However, "pluralization, defined ideologically, is where there are a competing number of worldviews available to members and no one world view is dominant…[and this is where the trouble comes in] if pluralism is extrapolated to mean relativism, then we are on a deadly course."[79]

Integration between many cultures introduces multiple religions into a society, wherein seekers of truth then have numerous options available. This can yield two dangerous results: 1) seekers, when overly convicted by the moral stance of a religious outline, simply depart in search of a more palatable truth; or 2) they absorb certain aspects of each religion and blend them into what they believe to be *their* truth, without commitment to any *one religion*, producing an autonomous moral code that comes from an internal infrastructure of preferences.

This is a slippery slope, and in our postmodern world, this "non-committal religious sampling" can create a false sense of religious security among those who are seeking a pleasanter version of truth with more easily defined rules and convictions. Additionally, it breeds a populace wherein each individual believes himself or herself so moral that he or she has evolved beyond the need for God. Beyond this, these individuals often teach "their truth" to seekers around them. This type of dabbling-but-never-committing activity soon produces a quasi-religious, anti-biblical frame of mind creeping into society. The results can be disastrous: a world in which no one has any real truth (nor does anyone want to commit to it), but in which all individuals are convinced that they *know* truth. Through this revolution of religious stance and eventual lack of convictions, society suffers a shortage of absolute reason—or moral criteria by which we reason absolutely. This is the point where pluralism changes from a strength-rendering asset for a nation to the source of conflict for many of its members.

PRIVATIZATION

When the open-ended, individual search for truth is taken into consideration with a society that has lost its capacity for shame or conviction, a role reversal occurs between those who used to make up the moral thread of a nation and those who used to isolate themselves because their morality was based on different criteria than the majority of society. (The version of this we are seeing right now is the transformation of a predominantly Christian society to a secularized, pluralized, postmodern one in which biblical statements are labeled as "hate speech.") A culture that has lost shame and aptitude for absolute moral reasoning forces the next stage that Ravi Zacharias cites as an important revolution that happened in the 1960s and that came as a result of secularization and pluralization: privatization. The word "privatize" is defined: "to make private; especially: to change from public to private control or ownership."[80] In this instance, the word refers to the need for seclusion within a society with an adapted sense of conviction and likewise whose criteria for absolute moral reasoning has become skewed. As a result, individuals with previously elevated values become a minority and therefore retreat into isolation. In a former state of society, religious morality was a foundation of social acceptance and those with lifestyles that contradicted those principles withdrew as a result of the influence of the common moral thread. But in a society that doesn't relegate typical behavior to religious principles, and one in which shame (or conviction) is dismissed until it is no longer an obstacle for an individual, the majority moves in an anti-moral direction. Statements of morality are then met by the mainstream crowd with hostility. Then, those who act upon absolute morality dictated by religious conviction are considered "old-fashioned," "misfits," or even "politically incorrect."

Their statements are considered "hate speech." The effects of this can be seen throughout society in large and small ways, and, as stated earlier, affect everybody, regardless of personal religious stance, because the majority dictates what is "normal" or "acceptable."

Some examples of this are happening around us even now. Nativity scenes during the holidays, once visible across the landscape during the Christmas season, are now the subject of debate and even attack, and are often met with demands for removal. Courses in our public schools often teach principles from non-Christian religions for the sake of "education," but any biblical teachings, even for historical purposes, quickly cause scandal or are removed from the curriculum. Even the simplest personal freedoms—such as wearing a Christian-themed T-shirt to public workplaces or posting a Christian faith statement on social media—fall under attack. The list goes on and on.

Zacharias likewise explains the devastating effects of privatization on the individual who is searching for meaning and purpose, but who is not allowed to connect these attributes with faith:

> In the spiritual world; in the world of your faith and your belief; [which is] your connectedness in the deepest confines of your soul…if they are relegated only to the private, it is an amputation and breaks away your connection with meaning. [The ramifications are] Secularization: no shame. Pluralization: no reason. Privatization: no meaning.

The danger of a society that exists within this realm, according to Zacharias, is that when personal convictions, based on moral absolutism, must be privatized, we begin to forfeit the right to personal meaning because these elements are intrinsically connected within our inner being. Our moral code, made of that which is dearest to our hearts—our convictions, our faith, our belief in a higher power, even essential building blocks for our very identity—is surrendered, a casualty of the pressure of living in a society that frowns upon our beliefs. Of this isolation of personal conviction, Zacharias says: "Privatization leads you ultimately where you are compelled in your spirit to sever your ties with your deepest commitment of the soul, and relegate it to the private world: [because] you daren't bring it into the public world."[81]

THE DESIRE FOR COMMUNITY

One of the strongest descriptors of our young generations is their passion for community. We see the word "community" plastered across articles and slogans referencing Millennials. When members of this group are asked what they really want, "community" is one of their leading responses, yet the *New York Post* recently released an article explaining that 64 percent[82] of Millennials feel disconnected from their neighbors and 22 percent[83] do not know any of their blockmates. Even so, 72 percent[84] reported feeling greater happiness when connected to a community. In light of these numbers, it appears that many young adults believe they would enjoy being involved in an assemblage: to them, the concept of community represents something alluring. However, many are disconnected from their neighborhoods, and a significant number are strangers to those who live nearby. This lends credibility to the idea that, perhaps, when Millennials say the word "community," they are talking about something more significant than good standing with those who live on their street. This, then, prompts the question: What is "community" to a Millennial?

Without much searching, we quickly discover that the young generation believes "community" involves "sensing belonging to a social group...[that is] not exclusive anymore: people can opt to identify with any number of different communities, rather than the one that they are born into."[85] So, this is not a geographical concept. This may go without saying to those who have had or witnessed involvement with online societies. However, author Shirley Le Penne makes a vital connection: "For Millennials, nominally joining a community does not automatically mean belonging to it. And not having that strong sense of belonging often compensates itself in feeling obliged to personally impact the world."[86]

What a fascinating association. When young people lacking a sense of belonging (perhaps due to being isolated, anxious, and fatherless?) join a collective and don't find what they're seeking, they become personally motivated to make a change in the world (does this sound like a Millennial to you?). Furthermore, Le Penne continues: "Modern society has shaped the art of making people feel dispensable.... Millennials understand belonging to a community as an opportunity to reverse this tendency: pursuing a sense of belonging becomes a means of achieving a sense of being needed."[87] She explains that through this type of involvement, one becomes aware of others' needs and develops a sense of belonging by meeting the necessities of others—which makes that person feel valuable, or *indispensable*. Out of this development comes the knowledge that one has valuable contributions, and thus, *belongs*. Furthermore, the person is not easily replaced, forgotten, or abandoned. This type of psychological, social, and emotional security is precisely what Millennials are asking for when they say they are seeking to be involved in a community. Beyond this, as the person carves out a unique place in the surrounding population, the collective accomplishes things—together—and the individual is thus linked to actions and benefits that are bigger and farther reaching than his or her efforts alone. This affiliation with a movement larger than any one person's influence drives an individual's sense of destiny, which we will discuss a little later in the book. Beyond all of this, Le Penne reminds us that, as these connections are fortified, the individual wakes up one day to find that, along the way, he or she has built lasting, deep relationships with others.

LINGUAL SABOTAGE

Why is it, then, that when young people use the word "community," what they're asking for is slightly different than the word itself, which conveys the idea that people know their geographical neighbors or some other, shallower, endeavor? Instead, why doesn't a Millennial simply say, "I'm looking to interact with a group of people wherein I can find identity and purpose"? This is a good question, but I see this type of scenario unfolding throughout our language. I call this dilemma "lingual sabotage," and I believe it is a product of a twofold conundrum.

First, many of our youth haven't learned the same way as older generations to consider a single point on a serious, in-depth level over a period of time, and then effectively articulate it through language. This statement may initially make Millennials defensive, but hear me out. Our youth are brilliant, intelligent people, but their communication skills have been shaped by different influences than those shaping the communication skills of the age groups who have gone before. Due to the intrusion of media—which will be covered more thoroughly later in this book—young adults often struggle when the time comes to deeply and thoroughly consider and relay one thought train. However, today's youth are much better at multitasking than many older people, which is likewise a product of the media's involvement in their brain development. *They* know what others their own age mean when they say these things, but older folks, whose minds process ideas and communicate them a different way, often need a fuller, less abbreviated explanation in order to grasp what the youths are really asking for. Because of this, many demands made by the young (and departing) audience regarding today's churches have been responded to with the wrong methods. Exasperated church leaders often find that they have done *precisely what they thought was requested of them*, yet they didn't do what *their young members wanted at all.*

Second, many times, the media uses key words to represent a complex, multifaceted collection of ideas, concepts, or trends that then are all summed up with the one word. The generation raised under the influence of our current media naturally follows suit. Quickly, and without intention, words like "community" are coined to represent a deeper connection of concepts. This is also shown through words such as "identity," "acceptance," and "tolerance," to name only a few. Often, these words place people on guard, when the *real* concept behind them is much more complicated and even *positive*. I'll elaborate on lingual sabotage more throughout the book as examples surface.

Through lingual sabotage, people often become defensive due to the introduction of certain words into a conversation. Many of these words, because they don't accurately communicate the intended point and because they are often confrontational, set people at odds before the conversation is finished, causing division from the start: hence, the phrase "lingual sabotage."

DIVISIVE INDOCTRINATION

Another type of sabotage of our youth is the concept that "diversity" means "division." True, both words derive from the root "divide," yet a crowd can have a diverse population and maintain a unified purpose. The concept that friction is being impressed upon our youth is contrary to their wish for community, subverting their aspirations of enjoying community. The result is an underlying tension between what people deem to be "factions" in a world where, in actuality, the Millennials want no part of *factional division*. The ensuing conflict creates anxiety so subtle that many cannot put their finger on its source.

Consider the statement made by Evan Osborne of the *Quillette*, who summed up this conundrum as follows:

Such people tend to assume a list of cultures (subject to change through political pressure) and argue that these are intrinsically different, and that preserving these differences is not just important but vital.... In other words, diversity is yet another thing to be managed, rather than something continuously evolving and best left alone.... Historically, cultures everywhere have improved by borrowing liberally from one another through commerce, colonialism, and mere curiosity. But although the diversity ideology is promulgated most aggressively by self–identified "progressives," it is in fact a reactionary dogma which insists cultures need to be defended from pressures to evolve and from the influence of alternative modes of thought and behavior. Instead, any permissible contact with people in other cultures must be mediated by a credentialed expert, usually a member of the culture to be protected.[88]

The damage from such manipulative tactics produces an undertone of confusion for our youth. Media, political movements, and social trends everywhere call one and all to rally for similar causes; however, once the crowd arrives, "mediators" come on the scene to organize people into—and represent—factions. How is a young person supposed to experience community when the congregation is both assembled and separated within the same day? Yet, as previously mentioned, the tactic is so subtle that the sabotage is seldom recognized. Friction mounts from an ambiguous, unseen source, and individuals are further isolated without understanding why.

Osborne offers another helpful insight:

Most recently, this attempt to promote cultural autarky has metastasized into a stern and inflexible opposition to "cultural appropriation," the belief that cultures are owned by specific people, and that no one in another cultural silo even have the right to enjoy the practices of other cultures unguided, still less alter them.... Cultural protectionism is harmful because successful societies are always in motion.[89]

It may seem that I am now contradicting what I stated previously about pluralization, but my point here is different. The pluralization of religious values can be dangerous, because when relativism enters the picture, religions are often watered down by individuals as they see fit, leaving them with no moral convictions other than those written both *by* and *for* themselves. This is perilous, because human beings need a higher standard on which to hinge morality, as stated previously. However, the danger of divisive indoctrination is the fact that *socially* and *culturally*, this country (and increasing regions throughout the world) has already blended. The division of what is unified is counterproductive. Therefore, when we call our youth together in an "all for one, one for all" manner and insert "experts" who become guardians of various factions, the contradiction both confuses and impedes societal harmony.

Political journalist, commentator, and author Heather MacDonald takes this concept a step further by stating that "from the moment students step foot on a college campus they are surrounded by a preposterous ideology that tells them to think of themselves as either the oppressed, which is a highly prestigious position to be in, or the oppressor."[90] This is only one of many examples of how, upon arrival into what should otherwise be a positive community-oriented setting, division is immediately sown.

THESE PEOPLE ARE ACTIVISTS

Perhaps now that we know a little bit more about a Millennial's desire for community, we may more easily see the connection to increased political activism amongst our youth. *Vice Impact's* Derrick Feldmann observes that "Millennials possess the ability to organize, drive awareness and influence the behavior of other generations through vast social media networks, with an ease and to a degree this country has never seen."[91] *Mic Network's* David Burstein claims that Millennials are in fact more effective activists than Baby Boomers were during the 1960s, stating that their "activism is even more powerful, more suited for the time we are living in, and in the long term, more sustainable."[92] Beyond this, Burstein says that Millennials are even more powerful because of their vast technological skills, their ability to influence movements both online and offline, and their motivation to create organizations and businesses to create ripples "where our political process seems too gridlocked to take decisive action."[93] The Millennial influence is so prominent that even large corporations are changing political statements to keep favor with the young masses. "Many executives recognize that today's youth will also become their main customers in the future, and are taking a new stand on some of these socio-political issues. According to new research from Sprout Social, 66% of consumers find it important for brands to speak out on [political] issues."[94]

Unfortunately, there is a potential caveat to the Millennials' enthusiasm for getting behind a cause. Although they may be clamoring to support a movement, their involvement may not be in their best interest. Many trends have successfully swept away the passions of young people, sometimes leading them down life roads that are not constructive. Furthermore, recall that with secularization and privatization, people who begin feeling that their efforts are valued or appreciated may then privatize any conviction or disagreement they harbor toward a particular movement, opting instead to believe they have made the world a better place through their valuable contributions. Our young generation is full of intelligent, passionate people, but make no mistake: They, being human, are still capable of being played. This is the paradox of the fervor of youth: If wholesome and beneficial opportunities are not available, dubious causes will arise to meet that young person's need to get involved in pushing for change.

Could it be that as individuals created in the image of God, these people are hardwired to see good works take place and don't want to miss the chance to be part of a movement?

Perhaps Millennials are innately aware of what Ephesians 2:10 has been telling us all along: "For we are his workmanship, created in Christ Jesus unto good works, which God hath before ordained that we should walk in them."

THE DAMAGE OF ISOLATION

As our young population suffers the isolation that has many sources—the breakdown of family, the increasing geographical distance between relatives, lingual sabotage, divisive indoctrination, lack of community, and more—it becomes more understandable why they are labeled the most isolated generation to date. This is related to, but much deeper than, regular loneliness. In fact, one definition of the word "isolation" is "an individual socially withdrawn or removed from society."[95] Over long periods, this has profound impact on a person.

Consider the story of Roy Petitfils, who was so obese that, when he was sixteen, his mother was forced to take him to a butcher to stand on a Toledo meat scale in order to obtain an accurate weight for his medical doctor, whose professional scale only went up to 350 pounds. When the scale registered 454 pounds, Roy and his mother agreed that they had to do something. But how had he arrived at this point in the first place? Like 34 percent of his generation, he had been born in a single-parent household, and like so many others in such households, he was exposed to poverty as a child. His mother, determined to give him her best, worked up to four jobs at a time to keep him in private school because of her determination to help her son have a fuller repertoire of resources than she herself had. The consequence of this well-meaning endeavor on this honest, hard-working woman's part was that Roy was intensely isolated. He reported that when he was twelve, he would wait at home alone for his mother to arrive and would often cry himself to sleep out of loneliness—but with the conflicted awareness that her absence was a testament to her love for him.

Roy recalls: "I began numbing the pain with food. And like any addict will tell you, it just took more and more of what didn't work to make the pain go away."[96] As he perpetually gained more weight during the rest of his teen years, the social pressure of attending a private school, where many peers were well-dressed and accomplished, further drove him into seclusion. The situation escalated until he was bullied and cruelly made fun of, isolated while he was "unmercifully picked on through school."[97] It became a normal practice during this season for the young man to pray at night that he would not wake up the next morning. When the shaming from his peers finally decreased, it was because instead of receiving negative attention, he began to receive none at all. This brought momentary relief, but after a while, he felt so ignored and forgotten that he came to a conclusion that shaped his entire life: "Unlike many in pop-psychologies say, rejection is not our greatest fear. Our greatest fear is to be invisible."[98]

A life-changing turn of events came about for Roy when he began to attend a Catholic college, wherein he was befriended by several people. Despite his weight, they invited him into their inner circle, and through the influence of their friendship, he built relationships that have lasted through today. He lost nearly three hundred pounds and even met the young woman who would later become his wife. Petitfils asserts that the message he wishes to deliver through his story is that it may seem that his triumph was found in victory over poverty or obesity, but the issue was deeper than this. In his words: "The challenge I overcame, I overcame with people who *saw me*. Who helped me to realize that I wasn't invisible."[99] He explains that while teenagers' problems may be hidden beneath more visible symptoms—such as his were with weight and economic status—the more profound desire of youth today is to be *seen*.

Young people want to be connected to others through *real* relationships—particularly with adults. Isolation is a form of loneliness that runs much deeper than rejection and leads to hopelessness that makes people feel that they are alone in the world. When people are exposed to short seasons of such conditions and have enough life experience to understand that the pain is situational or temporary, and supportive relationships are present, they can maneuver through these troubled times. But when youth who are positioned within a society that carries a continual undertone of adversity have few or no relationships they can call upon for help, their hope is diminished.

Isolated long enough, people become particularly vulnerable to suicidal thoughts. Consider the statement made by Mark Henick, who wrestled with this struggle throughout his teen years. "I was barely a teenager this first time I tried to kill myself. If I knew then what I know now; well, it probably wouldn't have changed very much.... Sometimes it doesn't matter what you *know*, what you *feel* just takes over."[100] Why such a statement? Henick explains that at this time, his perception had been limited. In fact, he takes this notion a step further by stating that the limitations of our insight are set into place by our "biology, by our psychology, [and] by our society. These are the factors which create that bubble which surrounds us. That is our perceptual field: our world as we know it."[101] During the navigation of this "bubble," Henick says, he came to view himself as: "You're not good enough, you're not smart enough, you're not *enough*."[102] The deadly problem with isolation is that when people begin to believe this lie, there is often no one around to tell them otherwise—or at least nobody they are capable of hearing in their moment of acute pain.

Long-term isolation is the experience of many young people today. If there is any doubt, revisit some of the phrases coined to label this generation and consider them alongside the statistics given at the beginning of this book. Doubt will likely be quickly dispelled. These trends, combined with the lingual sabotage and negative, divisive indoctrination that our youth are continually barraged with, have made this type of loneliness the norm for such young people, and society sends a clear, continual message that floats just beneath the surface:

You are all alone.

3

THE IDENTITY CRISIS

"*WHO* ARE YOU?" is a question that begins a quest.

"*What* are you?" is a question that prompts crisis, because it strips away identity and personhood.

As a side effect of the many cultural and moral revolutions discussed in the previous chapter, the concept of personal identity amongst our youth has become a matter of conflict. Contrary to the way previous generations grew up with a more secure sense of self-identity—and thus were more empowered to plan what they would do with their own lives—Millennials suffer an onslaught of individuality questions that derail their ability to dream of such luxuries as destiny, meaning, purpose, and legacy. Instead of being able to explore the question of *who* they are and *what they will do with their lives*, they face issues such as *what they identify as* and *how they will prove it*.

"Identity," as it pertains to living beings, is defined as "the distinguishing character or personality of an individual; the relation established by psychological identification; sameness of essential or generic character in different instances, sameness in all that constitutes the objective reality of a thing: oneness."[103] The problem with using a dictionary to define "identity" is that it is a concept so rooted in an individual's soul that it is nearly impossible to break down beyond a series of nuances. This is easier for Christians than for non-Christians, because when we experience a loss, we deviate toward Scripture or other spiritual, biblical principles from which we borrow concepts of our own identity. Understanding that we are made in the image of God (Genesis 1:27) often makes it easier to accept certain attributes that nonbelievers may be unable or unwilling to account for.

For example, people who believe they are made in God's likeness and see themselves as adopted sons or daughters (2 Corinthians 6:18) may chalk up their talents and strengths as an endowment from the Lord (Ephesians 2:10), their desires as dreams instilled by their Creator to drive them toward destiny (Joel 2:28), and their shortcomings as areas in which God is still working (Philippians 1:6). The true concept of personhood cannot be chosen overnight, nor can it be borrowed from a trending social or political movement. Legitimate, innate identity is a complicated combination of many attributes—some inherited from parent personality styles and others ingrained during the young and malleable stages of infanthood and childhood. Other elements come into play as a person ages into adolescence and adulthood. The most important components, however, are within every human being from the moment of conception and derive from our direct connection to our Maker: His image. Therefore, the farther we deviate *from* Him, the deeper our disconnection from this important element of self becomes.

Like everything else, the more society migrates away from the order that God has set for us, the more frantically we scramble to fill the emptiness left by this disconnection from His plan. The result is a dissatisfying, unfulfilling substitution for what was initially intended for us. Unfortunately, the modern identity crisis is one of the ways our youth have been robbed of a stronger connection to their destiny. Furthermore, the word "identity" itself has become another form of lingual sabotage, in that its very mention immediately places people on guard even though in its purest form, "identity" is a beautiful thing.

IT'S BIGGER THAN ORIENTATION

The conversation about identity is at times intertwined with that of LGBTQ (lesbian, gay, bisexual, transgender, queer) rights and relationships, especially in the media. However, the question of true identity is a deeper issue than many initially perceive, and indeed it encompasses profoundly more than sexuality. In fact, questions regarding sexual orientation and gender identity are *byproducts* of the deeper question of *true identity*. After all, there are many aspects of people besides the technicalities by which they sexually identify. For this reason, the conversation regarding identity is immensely vaster than that of orientation. The query runs much deeper, and it is that core, central element that this book will attempt to address. The topic is so clouded in our society that the concept is misrepresented—even abbreviated— often both *to* and *by* individuals who believe they've answered the question about their own identity.

For example, people who choose to identify as women (such as myself, as I was born female) may, because of the messages sent out in today's media, believe this means they've entirely settled the matter of their identity. But, the concept of *who I am as an individual* is much more deeply ingrained into my innermost being than can possibly be answered with the simple words, "I'm a woman." Additionally, I might at times find it offensive, even degrading, for others to assume they understand my entire identity structure simply because they are aware that I was born female and generalized as such: "She's just like all the other women," or "Female drivers!" Those approaching the orientation/LGBTQ conversation from all angles likely agree with me on this point.

Thus, how people choose to identify in terms of the modern gender-sexual orientation movement is, as stated previously, a result of a deeper-rooted identity that is seeded inside people over their entire lives. It is a complex structure influenced by religion, upbringing, moral code (presented to a child and reinforced through teen and adult years), self-esteem, cultural interactions and experiences, and contributions made by the individual in roles such as family, community, society, the professional world, and even church. As each season comes and goes, layers of this awareness are added, refined, and developed more fully. Out of the growth and shaping of true, *inner* identity spring the answers to such questions as how someone *externally* identifies to the rest of the world. Even many who profess their distinctiveness through orientation or gender identification are likely to acknowledge the validity of this statement. Hence, the conversation about LGBTQ is not directly pertinent to the *core issue of identity,* but is rather *a reflection of the individual's deeper state and condition.* This said, this book will not tackle the issues involved in the LGBTQ movement, because we believe that when the deeper questions of identity are recognized and answered, the question of sexual orientation and gender identity iron themselves out on an individual basis between a person and God.

While much of the world seems to migrate directly to questions of sexual identity and orientation at the very mention of the word "identity" (again, lingual sabotage), there are in fact many nonsexual ways a person can externally identify that stem from the truer, deeper developed sense of self. Unfortunately, in our current media, many of these other elements, such as nationality, ethnicity, race, culture, religion, and even language, dialect, disability, and professional status[104] (and this list is certainly not exhaustive), take a backseat to the sexual component. As a result, the word "identity" itself has been misrepresented to our youth—during the very years when they are attempting to sort the matter out personally. Because of this, many young people truncate their search for their personal identity by limiting their quest to the matter of sexual orientation. Often, sadly, they become unaware that they are on a much deeper and more involved journey than that.

It Must Work from the Inside Out

Our sense of self must be brought out of who we perceive ourselves to be within the world, how we view our contributions on both large and small scales, our self-esteem, and even the roles we play when interacting with others. As this sense of self develops, it's natural to direct it outward to the surrounding world. The results can be either beneficial or detrimental, depending on the quality of experiences that transpire during development, but manifestations of identity roles are visible throughout our population. I would wager that most of the stances we take or statements we make are a reflection of our identity. Beyond this, more ambiguous factors (such as feeling powerless or unequal) can contribute to the sense of identity, and sometimes even cause a self-inflicted state of entrapment. For example, we've likely all known someone who seems to be continually stuck in "victim mode:" a form of identity misplacement caused by a lack of perceived self-empowerment. An illustration of this would be a youth whose only aspiration is to live a lifestyle centered on crime because it's all he or she knows, or a youngster who is determined to attend a certain university—not because it's best for his or her career plan, but because previous generations of the family attended there. Other types of identity-role manifestations can include bullying, timidity, strong leadership, people-pleasing, or carrying out acts of benevolence and charity. More important than including an extensive list of identity manifestation types in this book will be to thoroughly explain the long-term importance of a balanced, fully developed individuality, and to likewise emphasize that the current identity politics surrounding sexuality don't begin to address the *true nature of what a person needs to discover when attempting to establish distinctiveness.* Furthermore, misplacements of identity are harmful in that they serve as distractions that rob our youth from the opportunity to establish a stronger sense of self and destiny.

Unfortunately, our world often embraces the external qualities of what people believe their identity to be instead of recognizing them as characteristics of the deeper self. Next, that image is imposed on others as though it is their fully developed character. For example, a young person who is caught stealing may begin to be regarded—by both himself/herself and by peers—as nothing more than a thief. In light of this, he or she may migrate into a life of crime as a result of misplaced identity. Thus, the question of true individuality becomes skewed—and worse, causes the person to miss the mark and never completely answer the biggest inward questions at all. The result is that the person is left with deep-rooted inquiries that can go unresolved for a lifetime, contributing to a sense of emptiness that is never satisfied.

WHAT IS IDENTITY?

When misconceptions allow us to believe that identity is constructed *from* our external statements or attributes (political, racial, religious, or otherwise), instead of helping us recognize that these come from the uniqueness *within us,* two negative situations arise within our easily-influenced, identity-pursuing youth: 1) Questions connected to individuality are routed through the channels of external attributes and statements, essentially "misplacing" the underlying problem and possibly driving them to choose destructive life routes, and 2) Deep-seeded characteristics and qualities that *should* be the source of identity are overlooked, and they are robbed of a deeper concept of their own distinctiveness brought about by their aspirations, dreams, destiny, and legacy.

These essentials (aspirations, dreams, destiny, and legacy) must be brought back to the forefront of the topic at hand. Somewhere along the way, they have been tossed to the wayside of this conversation, and thus the vital elements of identity are often missing. The individual likely *feels* their absence, but is unable to articulate where the inner conflict lingers unresolved. Everyone, however, has the need to develop a sense of distinction that springs from the answers to core questions they have about themselves. These are questions such as:

- Where do I belong in the world?
- How do I fit into my extended family and even my community to play a unique and crucial contributing role?
- What do my peers think of me? What type of reputation do I have with those around me?
- Am I a good citizen, and do I positively contribute to the world around me?
- Do my negative experiences and painful memories define who I am and who I will be?
- If I have done bad things in the past, can I still change my life's path so that I can become a good person who contributes positively to society?
- What will I do with my life?
- Was I born with a purpose derived from my abilities, talents, skills, and interests?
- What are my life's dreams?
- Do I have a unique destiny that only I can fulfill?
- Can I leave a legacy for future generations to benefit from?
- If I were no longer on this earth, would others feel my absence?
- If the answer to the previous question is yes, *how* would others feel my absence? Would I leave behind a vacancy that no other individual could fill?
- Is there a God, and does He know or care who I am?
- If there is a God, did He create me with a specific purpose?
- If there a God, does He love me?

The Evolution of the Concept

During the premodern era and the early part of the modern era, many of these questions were answered for a child at birth. In a culture with fewer options, an individual's path was often revealed as he or she grew up. For example, a family's last name often described their profession—and thus likely foretold a child's future profession as well. For example, names such as Clark, Mason, Potter, Taylor, or Weaver referred to families of a scribe ("clerk"), a stoneworker, a maker or seller of pottery, a person who makes or repairs clothing, and a person who makes cloth, respectively.[105] Others, such as Brooks, Greenwood, or Perry—just to name a few—correlated with the family's geographical location,[106] while names such as Sutton, Hamilton, Bedford, or Hampshire noted a family's proprietorship of land or notable estate in a specific area.[107] Beyond this, first names were traditionally handed down through families; only in recent decades have parents migrated away from this method of baby-name choosing, opting instead to select names they simply like.

Birth names represent only one example of how a worldwide cultural shift impacts an individual's sense of identity onset at birth. In generations past, marriages were often arranged far in advance by families who chose life mates for their children based on political or material security rather than affection. In many cultures, education (if offered at all) was limited to the basic daily essentials for survival, after which teaching life skills often took the place of formal classroom education, further carving out a child's position in society. Similarly, a culture with fewer necessities and amenities than many of us enjoy today (such as food, clean drinking water, medical provision, and material wealth) placed mere survival at higher priority than more developed cultures. As a result, extended questions of one's identity, life goals, and even destiny weren't analyzed with the complexity with which they are today, and for many in previous generations, concepts of life-path preference or happiness were luxuries afforded by few.

"IDENTITY'S" TRUE IDENTITY

Erik Erikson (1902–1994), famous for his theories of stages of psychosocial development, was a German-American psychologist and psychoanalyst noted for originating and mapping a series of junctures that he introduced as the developmental phases in each stage of life. Unlike previous influential figures within the world of psychological science (such as Sigmund Freud, who placed a high focus on psychosexual development), Erikson focused on psychosocial elements within the human mind.

During the early childhood phase (ages two through six), Erikson explains, the conflict everyone faces is something he called "initiative versus guilt." Laura E. Berk, professor of psychology at Illinois State University and author of such college-level textbooks as *Development Through the Lifespan, Child Development,* and *Infants, Children, and Adolescents,* elaborates: "As the word *initiative* suggests, young children have a new sense of purposefulness," she says. "They are eager to tackle new tasks, join in activities with peers, and discover what they can do with the help of adults. They also make strides in conscience development."[108] Beyond this, children begin to develop a sense of self-awareness as related to their attributes, attitudes, abilities, and values that help them nurture a healthy self-view.[109] Early definitions of self are tied to the primary concepts of self-esteem, which are vital to psychological adjustment as it pertains to emotional adaptation, behavioral learning, and long-term demeanor.[110] During this period, children form and explore attachment to caregivers and they make-believe play with other children. The appropriate amount and type of care, coaching, and discipline are vital for the development of self-esteem and identity. Digital and media interference, often unbeknownst to well-meaning parents, causes a desensitization that interferes with a child's attachment to others, thus interrupting integration into the surrounding community. This will be covered at more length in a later chapter. For now, suffice to say, the formation of self-esteem and identity is well underway even during the earliest years of life.

Erikson describes the developmental conflict of middle childhood (ages six through eleven) as something called "industry versus inferiority." Berk explains that this phase "is resolved positively when experiences lead children to develop a sense of competence at useful skills and tasks."[111] This is the chapter when children begin to look beyond their own little world to seek meaningful placement within the culture and community around them. Likewise, Erikson identifies inferiority as detrimental to a child's development and explains that a "positive but realistic self-concept, pride in accomplishment, moral responsibility, and cooperative participation with age-mates"[112] are vital for refining the forming identity in middle childhood. Furthermore, research shows that during this season, a child's self-esteem does not directly benefit from overindulgent compliments such as "you're great" that are unrelated to a skill or an accomplishment. Instead, building a child's positive self-image is successfully fostered through setting and achieving worthwhile goals.[113] Throughout this, a cyclical growth occurs. Self-esteem is built by accomplishing valuable actions, and these successes bolster the confidence necessary to elevate goals and strive further.[114] Thus, compliments that resonate deeply to a child during this phase of development point out a strength, attribute, talent, or ability: "You are extremely good at math. I hope you know you are very smart," or "Thank you for helping Sally with her books. You are a very kindhearted person, and the world needs more people like you."

To truncate a complex study (which could be its own book, and remains the sole purpose of hundreds of other books), we can nutshell the statement as follows: During middle childhood, children become more aware of the world around them and derive self-esteem and a strong sense of identity from believing that they have a unique, vital, contributive role in it. This belief underwrites further effort toward those means, which fosters a sense of self-accomplishment, in turn validating the belief that they have an irreplaceable and essential purpose here on earth.

As children mature and enter adolescence, their identity shifts again and begins to solidify. Building blocks laid during the early and middle childhood years provide a foundation upon which a new layer is added. As stated earlier, the identity derived during this stage is partially built out of the attachment to early caregivers and partially from religious, political, geographical, and ethnic thoughts and attitudes obtained from the family. Additional development is seen in the areas of self-esteem, pride in achievement, placement within the community, and the vitality of one's role in the community—all of which the child is attempting to address through the industry-versus-inferiority stage of middle childhood. During adolescence, however, these issues become more personal. Potential family or community roles become increasingly centered around the individual and begin to hint at life goals or aspirations. Middle childhood thoughts such as "I am helpful to my mom in the kitchen, and she appreciates me," or "My dad really valued my help raking leaves" morph into adolescent thoughts such as "I could become a chef" or "Someday I'd like to own my own landscaping business."

When identity is constructed this way, it takes place organically over the course of a person's life. However, when identity questions are rerouted toward external attributes that people are expected to quickly choose and then "identify" as—especially when the individuals are very young—it places great pressure on children to answer questions that their minds haven't even cognitively answered. This goes deeper than what many people think of when it is said that a child is not ready to "answer certain questions"—it is possible that brain development literally has not yet reached that stage. As children grow and their brains' cognitive abilities cultivate, there is a natural order to identity development that, when presented in reverse, the child simply is not prepared to take on. We can compare this idea to asking a child to do multiplication before his or her brain has developed enough to even process basic addition. The child will either be overwhelmed by the question and begin to withdraw or try to "bluff" a correct answer. (Children may eventually even convince *themselves* that the answer is correct, even if it isn't.) Worse, the younger and more easily influenced the child, the more susceptible he or she is to peer pressure, yielding the increased possibility that he or she will adjust her position based on a desire to please others rather than on personal conviction. Considering this, any statement the child might make that goes against what seems to be the trending majority or that results in negative feedback could result in forming the early habit of privatization. This can steer a child from a very young age to unknowingly compromise his or her sense of identity—or even his or her own moral code and conscience—in trade for what he or she perceives will be met with approval of others.

During adolescence, peer approval—along with social virtues—becomes increasingly important. Thus, how a person is viewed by others is increasingly prioritized, and is compounded by elements that others deem honorable, such as friendliness, kindness, cooperation, etc. Combining these things means that often, a teenager's self-esteem is directly fed by what others think, which is based on what the current, common morality clause and acceptable social nuances are. In this way, current social trends play a huge part—unbeknownst to our youth—in building the criteria that our youth defines as "self."

Erikson recognized that identity, under construction since birth, is the "major personality attainment of adolescence,"[115] and simultaneously named it as "a crucial step toward becoming a productive, content adult."[116] During this phase, Erikson names the conflict to be *identity versus role confusion*: the foundation for healthy development throughout this phase is determined and designed or undermined by success experienced during earlier childhood. Thus, early negative outcomes hinder future interactions, and a child deprived of the opportunity to explore within safe and nurturing parameters can develop attributes that later in life appear as though the individual is "shallow, directionless, and unprepared for the challenges of adulthood."[117] (This places new insight on some of our young adults of today, whose identities have been so barraged and who likewise face the very same accusations from an older, critical crowd). As already noted, the construction of identity becomes more central to the individual during adolescent years. The question of role within family and community remains, but is now weighed against values, beliefs, talents, and desires as well. The merging of these equally compelling counterparts determines the direction a person chooses to go in matters of education, family, career, community service, cultural and ethnic participation, and more. As a person weighs the reality of his or her own talents, abilities, and interests against the potential roles to fill within the community, the truest sense of self begins to form, out of which other decisions are made.

Culture plays a larger role in this than is often recognized. For example, in the premodern era, an "identity crisis" was practically unheard of. As options were few and choices were limited, people selected their roles fairly quickly, and life carried on. Deeper analysis was a luxury in many settings where survival was the center of communal efforts. The more multifaceted a culture, the more complex identity development can be, and the easier it is to inventory all the options and even feel overwhelmed. Add to this the removal of deep-rooted family tradition, religious influence, and absolute moral grounding throughout the preceding years, and a young adult may feel downright lost. A further complication (which will be covered later in the book) is created when so many young adults complete their education saddled with a large amount of debt, sowing maximum financial pressure into a life they may suddenly feel unprepared to succeed in. Their response can likely be one of two polar opposites: bravado and entitlement (sometimes viewed as narcissism) or withdrawal and disengagement (sometimes viewed as laziness). This could explain why many young adults today haven't yet had the courage to leave their parents' home (which will also be covered later in this book).

When identity formation goes well and individuals don't need to put on a brave front or withdraw, but see themselves as having true value with something to contribute and a unique and productive placement within the community, they psychologically adapt to a place of fully engaging in a fulfilling life and begin to evaluate a sense of destiny and legacy. These principles and allocations, formed throughout and solidifying toward the end of adolescence, serve as the foundation for a healthy, fruitful, and satisfying adult life.

Elements that play into individuals' self-esteem during childhood later serve as the "interconnecting fiber" that enables adults to feel ready to engage with the world, follow their dreams, and live according to the morality code embedded from childhood. Sadly, the opposite is true as well. Children raised with confusion, who are not compassionately nurtured or cared for, who don't have healthy interactions with peers, or who aren't given a gentle but firm code of morality from a young age can find themselves directionless and might even be viewed by others in a negative light. In this way, those who aren't given boundaries, interaction with positive and caring role models, healthy, skill-related compliments and encouragement, and even accomplishment-building responsibilities at a young age often are not prepared for the challenges of adulthood. Furthermore, children who are neglected at a young age or who lack sufficient positive interpersonal relations throughout childhood (a sweeping epidemic throughout the modern US brought on by overindulgence in technology, a subject that will be covered at length later in this book), are said by some experts to claim their identity in reverse—the *external* defines the *internal* rather than the other way around. For example, these individuals, due to not having a properly installed foundation over the formative years, tend to choose a trending identity and then follow through—something Berk describes as a sort of "process of exploration followed by commitment."[118]

There is a capricious type of pressure on young adults: the combination of looming imminent adulthood responsibilities alongside continual inquiry regarding future plans. For some, this becomes a powder keg of responsibilities both chosen and yet not undertaken thrust upon a person whose identity and community placement are still being tested and solidified. For some, choices are made and life's directions are initiated before consequences can be fully understood—whether it's a question of education, career, marriage and family, or even orientation. Beyond this, supportive and positive parents can partially fill the need for peer approval. However, when the family is uninvolved or even critical, the need for peer approval is redirected toward peers instead of toward trusted friends and family who may have had the individual's best interest in mind. As a result, friends alone, autonomous from the parental and family structure, gain extreme influence over the part of the core identity that is built by approval from others. Worse, often through adolescence and young adulthood, most peers are of similar age, development stage, and socioeconomic setting. Thus, the ideals, moral code, and even identity of those peers are likely still being formed as well, creating a scenario wherein one person's identity is impacted by another person (or group of people) who probably doesn't have any more life experience or wisdom than the individual.

How Does This Affect Our Youth?

The societal shift in development and placement of identity comes at great cost to our youth. The search for answers to certain questions within themselves (similar to those posed earlier in the chapter), such as "where do my talents and abilities fit into the world around me?" facilitates seeking, obtaining, and developing true, innate identity, wherein a person connects with a sense of unique destiny. This is a need all of us have within the deepest corners of our soul, whether we realize it or not.

Unfortunately, as stated previously, many have misconstrued the nature of innate identity, replacing the type that connects individuals with their destiny for a distracted, less-fulfilling substitution. The inability to build a legacy can lead Millennials to feel lost, without direction, out of place, or as though they have nowhere to belong, or that they are immensely lonely and even unloved. Anyone will acknowledge that basic human needs and desires involve such things as love and acceptance, a place to belong, a sense of family, and a sense of purpose. The modern identity crisis has sowed confusion into our youth's ability to develop the very attributes within their innermost being that answer the most important questions they have about themselves; this is a form of mental sabotage from the inside out.

WHERE IS THIS GOING?

For the sake of our study, it will benefit us to briefly look at the long-term ramifications of this distraction. We will fast-forward briefly to the final stages of Erikson's theory, *generativity versus stagnation*—wherein middle-aged adults begin to assess what they have left behind to contribute to future generations versus what they will withhold for themselves,[119] followed by the final stage—*ego integrity versus despair*—wherein senior-aged folks take a personal inventory of pride and regret regarding how their years were spent.[120] Generativity—the concept that one has left something behind for the benefit of future humanity—begins to grow in importance during middle adulthood and it escalates throughout the remaining years of life. This is wired into us from birth, but climaxes in importance the older we get. The opposite response, which is stagnation, is often the byproduct of regret. Stagnation turns our energies inward, as we withdraw from the desire to contribute to future societies (these individuals often hold a victimized mindset).

Generativity has been linked to those who are considered well-adapted parents with successful marriages and satisfying close friendships, and who live their later years with a greater sense of autonomy and a higher level of satisfaction.[121] In a seemingly cyclical fashion, generativity is reported to be more common within people who had or raised children than in those who did not.[122] In addition, generativity is reportedly higher among those who claim religious affiliation, and many whose ancestors suffered great persecution or poverty show extremely high levels of this trait, illustrating a desire to contribute to a world that migrates away from such occurrences and never returns.

During this phase, it is common for adults to want to mentor younger generations: to pass down life knowledge, guidance, and advice, and even impart warnings regarding lessons learned the hard way. Berk explains: "Increasing awareness of limited time ahead prompts adults to reevaluate the meaning of their lives, refine and strengthen their identities, and reach out to future generations."[123] This attribute serves as both a byproduct of and a generator of a fulfilling life, because it connects an individual with a strong sense of destiny and contribution to future civilization. A well-rounded, middle- or late-stage adult will be filled with compassion for young adults, which spawns the desire to sow seeds into them to help ease their journey through life. As this personal transformation takes place, it is only a continuation and maturation of that need to know and be known by others, to love and be loved, to contribute something unique to the world, to feel a sense of belonging, and ultimately, to give back before life is over.

This book focuses on the younger generations, but for our study, it has been important to discuss the concept of generativity within older adults for a few reasons. First, seeing what identity and generativity look like for an older adult sheds light on how some of our young adults are headed off-track and need our help. If their sense of self continues to develop without the proper grounding, they risk being increasingly depressed in their middle and late adulthood. The former stage is only several years away for the oldest Millennials, many of whom could reach another level of personal crisis based upon what they already lack. A deep need within our youth already goes unmet, courtesy of the current identity distraction. Every day that this "train" of our youth travels off-course, it meanders farther away from its intended destination. The ensuing vacancy does not go unnoticed, but rather causes those who already feel lost to, without realizing it, put their increasing efforts to establish a grounded sense of identity on the wrong track.

In short, many of our youth have been robbed of the opportunity to create and establish a fulfilling sense of destiny because of the distraction fostered by modern society. It costs them now, and, as we can see by following Erikson's theory about the later years in life, it will continue to cost these individuals as well as all of humanity.

THEN THEY ARE ATTACKED

Insult is added to injury when young people who are already in intense pain as a result of this "identity crisis" are further affronted by criticism of the older generations. In 2010, the *New York Post* ran a story characterizing youth in the workplace with the following words and phrases: "entitlement," "narcissism," "very inflated sense of self," "unrealistic expectations," "oversensitive," and "high maintenance." The article even called them "a chronic disappointment."[124]

As the parent of a Millennial and a Post-Millennial (and as a human being), it breaks my heart to see the persecution our young adults face from all directions. While it is true that our youth can, at times, appear to display some of these attributes, the friction created by the generation gap seems to manifest in acute resentment, which is entirely unproductive and doesn't help. After all, it is a well-established fact that members of our younger generation are "leaving the church in droves,"[125] and a mudslinging contest will not lead the lost back to Christ. The urgent condition of our youths' souls must be held at utmost priority. Beyond this, the challenges our young adults face, in many ways, are more puzzling than those dealt with in previous generations. While older folks *without doubt* confronted abysmal challenges within their own time, today's difficulties are so unique that there is not even yet a template for how to weather some of the current storms. This increases the isolation for our younger crowd who has to discern how to navigate these waters without the benefit of experience. Beyond this, when they are shunned and criticized by older generations who offer negative feedback rather than sympathy and guidance, the young become more lost, and the older do not benefit from their own positive participation, such as the previously described generative involvement engaged in by older individuals.

THE RUB

At this point, you may be thinking: *Younger generations don't want advice from older people. They've ignored it at every turn.* For some, this may indeed be the case. But, as we've already begun to discover, a deeper look at *what our young adults are asking for—in their own words*—often renders a different verdict. If this is the case, then mutual understanding and some effort on the part of *both generations* could create some common ground whereupon we could begin to rebuild societal bridges that are quickly being torn down.

Yet, another reason it is beneficial to understand the more progressive phases of identity that occur during the older years is this: By grasping the concept of generativity, we can pinpoint some of the friction between age groups, which derives partially from the passion by which older folks *want* to help the younger. As stated, generativity is particularly strong among individuals who claim a religious affiliation, have emerged from poverty, or descended from ancestry that was highly persecuted. A great percentage of the members of older generations within our society were deeply affected by World Wars I and II and the Great Depression of the 1930s. Even those who weren't yet alive during these events were raised by those who were, so the impact exists regardless of whether the individual is a Generation X-er, a Baby Boomer, or member of the Silent Generation (Boomers' parents). As a result, surveys have shown a high rating of generativity among these, particularly within the Baby Boom generation.[126]

This reveals that while our younger generation struggles with identity, destiny, and unprecedented problems, our older crowd is extremely impassioned about guiding them. I would wager that this desire is so intense that it often manifests in exasperation at unheeded advice. Each age bracket holds a set of unique assets and attributes, and can likewise be a force for good if we can find middle ground and work together to reunite.

TOLERANCE

A subversive and counterproductive concept has crept into our society's vocabulary: "tolerance." This is one example of the previously introduced notion of lingual sabotage. Before the reader thinks I'm preparing to say that the church needs to place a "smackdown" on people who don't agree with the Bible or see eye to eye with all of its principles, allow me to assure you that I'm coming from a different point of view. It's a perspective, in fact, that I borrow from Michael Ramsden, speaker and director at Wycliffe Hall of Oxford University, who spoke alongside Ravi Zacharias at the University of California at Los Angeles in 2013. In his explanation, Ramsden brought to light the fact that the word "tolerance," while presented in a positive light, tends to come attached to a negative connotation. He explained that it has become defined in modern settings to mean that we accept and agree with everyone around us. However, historically, when the word "tolerance" has been used, it denotes deviation. After all, individuals don't *tolerate* what they are like-minded on; they *agree with* it. However, the relationship between the two fosters the concept that one is passing moral or intellectual judgement upon another, which lends to friction. The result is the demand of something that we *perceive* to be positive, but inwardly *feel* is lacking.[127]

Ramsden goes on to use a hypothetical scenario to illustrate his point, wherein a person invites another out to a meal at a restaurant to visit—a proposal that is accepted. Later in this picture, a mutual friend asks the invitee if he enjoyed the meal out and if he appreciated the visit. If, in this hypothetical instance, the person who had been treated at the restaurant said, "Sure, it was tolerable," that would be extremely offensive to the individual who had initiated the get-together. Ramsden goes on to say, "I know very few people in this world who want to be tolerated, but I know a *lot* of people who want to be respected."[128]

The concept of tolerance has been born out of the human need to be accepted and loved *despite* differences. The very nature of the modern presentation of the word attempts to both unite and divide simultaneously. Unfortunately, the ramifications on our younger generations have been that, in an attempt to demand respect, additional controversy and discord have been sowed between sects, religious affiliations, and age brackets. As we all know, much more is involved in gaining respect than confrontationally demanding it. Yet, nobody wants to be disrespected for choosing to believe differently than those around them. Recall our discussion in the previous chapter regarding the transformation of philosophy from the premodern through the postmodern eras and into the current day. The evolution of philosophy over the centuries has brought the world to a place where many are exercising their prerogative to "declare their own truths." Unfortunately, simultaneously, many of these people attempt to ask for acceptance and love regardless of differing personal viewpoints, but mistakenly use the label of tolerance. When their demand is met simply as they made it and they are *tolerated*, subconsciously, they are keenly aware of what is missing and are thus left unsatisfied. Worse, when their demands are met with hostility, they feel rejected and unloved.

Again, this is an example of how our modern vocabulary has deviated from the core issue and replaced the central need with a negative, even confrontational, label, sowing discourse between and isolating people. Those who are frustrated with the conversation of "tolerance" may find themselves in a more compassionate state of mind by taking on a different perspective, realizing that, more often than not, those who are demanding "tolerance" from others are actually asking to be accepted and loved. Mentally interchanging these phrases as one listens to another will surely stir compassion and break barriers between factions.

FINDING THAT SILVER LINING

When discussing identity, we should also note briefly the issue of suffering and its impact on our constitution. This point is often belabored by older people who use such phrases as: "It's good for you to struggle; it builds character"; "What doesn't kill you will make you stronger"; and even a favorite at nearly any local church: "What doesn't make you bitter will make you better."

Often a young person's response is a placid smile, an eye roll, or even muttered accusations that the older person has no idea what it's like to suffer hardships. However, there is more than a modicum of truth to such claims. The older percentage of our culture, as stated before, were either directly, personally impacted by the World Wars and the Great Depression, or their parents were. As stated early on in this book, many claimed that it was their faith in God that got them through such hardships. Few will argue that even the strength of our nation was largely forged among the fires of adversity.

In a study conducted in France, two thousand adults were given a list of negative life events and surveyed about which of those they had experienced. The participants' emotional well-being, vulnerability to stressors, and mental health were initially assessed, then reassessed later in an effort to learn whether negative life events made them more or less resilient. Results indicated that, as long as the adversity was intermittent (not continuing for excessively long periods), exposure to difficult events contributed to the development of favorable traits, such as a stronger psychological ability to recover, better work and social resiliency, a decreased propensity for such conditions as post-traumatic stress disorder, and better overall satisfaction with life.[129]

This affirms that a personal sense of mastery is vital to healthy identity development in role manifestation. As people overcome hardship, they become aware of their own capabilities—not to mention that the inventory of individual strengths and weaknesses make people aware of their potential within the operation of community. Through this discovery, possible unique and vital contributions come to light, helping them shape future goals and dreams. Thus, a moderate amount of suffering builds resilience, contributes to identity and self-esteem, and even indirectly influences the ability to find one's place in this world. Furthermore, this builds a healthy answer to the question posed at the beginning of this chapter: "Who am I?" Through conquering obstacles, from somewhere deep within the self, the answer begins to emerge: "I am a survivor," "I am resourceful," or even "I am a future doctor/mother/teacher."

Furthermore, through adversity, many individuals find growth in personal faith, which lends to a sense of hope beyond one's own means.

A SIDE NOTE ABOUT RAVI ZACHARIAS

You may recall our discussion in the previous chapter of Ravi Zacharias, a Christian anthropologist, author, and speaker. Many don't know that when he was young, before he found his sense of purpose in truth-seeking and ministry, he was a hurting, seventeen-year-old boy who attempted suicide. What was the crux of the personal crisis that seemed so formidable that it made him willing to take his own life? He was lost and felt his life to be without meaning and purpose after failing at school. He was in intense emotional pain brought on by feelings of failure and decided he didn't want to continue on life's path. In a hospital bed after his suicide attempt, he began to read a Bible and then he came to know Christ. He explains that his search led him to four essential questions that everyone must answer:

Origin: where do I come from?
Meaning: what gives life meaning?
Morality: how do I differentiate between good and bad?
Destiny: what happens to human beings when they die?[130]

About these questions, Zacharias says, "You have to find answers that are correspondingly true to each of these questions, and all put together, it has to cohere."[131] John 14:19 says, "because I live, ye shall live also," and these words became a personal inspiration to Zacharias. "When Jesus came into my life," he said, "He didn't change *what I did, merely*, He changed what I *want to do*."[132]

The identity crisis facing our youth has, as stated, robbed them of their ability to assess their sense of personal dreams, destiny, and legacy. Furthermore, it has served as a wedge between a creation and its Creator. As Zacharias' revelation tells, when the lost reunite with God, their Maker, He prompts their journey into a new direction—one that leads to a true definition of self, imparts vision for the future, and unveils where they belong in the big picture.

Digital Orphans

A Generation Raised by Technology

From "It Takes a Village" to "It Takes a Tablet"

MANY MEMBERS OF the older generation generalize Millennials as an exasperating group of youngsters who cannot put down their phones. If, finally, a youth can be coerced into putting away the device away for a few minutes, a tablet or laptop soon takes its place. A clean break from technology for a little bit of quality conversation seems to be elusive when it comes to our youth. Even the phrase "face time," which would have previously insinuated a personal visit, now refers to a video chat over a variety of electronic means. To many seniors, this activity is hard to relate to and can even be a source of detachment/friction between age groups. Worse is the seeming night-and-day difference between the world today and that of only a few decades ago, when portable technology of any kind was considered extremely cutting-edge. Contrasting memories of that world with today's world in which every youngster carries at least one screen device makes it no wonder that many disdain this apparent need for and dependence on technology.

KIDS THESE DAYS

The oldest Millennials have reached their mid-thirties right now; thus, this is the first generation whose lives have largely been spent with access to technology. While it is true that many seniors fear change, it is likewise the case that the youngest generation *has lived under continual change— the likes of which the earth has never before seen.* Part of the friction between age groups, then, stems from the fact that many older people do not know *how* to handle these younger folks, because they represent and face challenges for which the world has—as of yet, as mentioned earlier—no template.

On this matter, Tedx Talks speaker Lindsey Pollak brings an interesting point to light, reminding her audience of the words of Hesiod in the eighth century BC: "I see no hope for the future of our people if they are dependent on the fruitless youth of today."[133] She follows this citation with her own comment: "We have literally been shaming our young people for all of human history."[134] Later in the same interview, she makes an essential argument for why young people seem to have the continual need to interface with technology:

> Millennials want to use the technology we have to work flexibly. Asking a Millennial, "Why are you always working on your device? Why are you always looking at your phone?" [Is]…kind of like asking a baby boomer "Why are you so into electricity? Why do you plug things in all the time? You always need an [electrical] outlet."

When you've come of age with that technology, you want to make use of it.[135]

While Millennials' seeming constant need to be enthralled in some sort of electronic device is one characteristic that frustrates many members of the older generations, it's possibly an unfair response considering

Pollak's statement. Yet, the question arises: How did we get here? Most middle- to older-aged adults remember when such devices didn't even exist, so the apparent need to be glued to one can seem like an off-putting, even rude, interruption to quality time with others. Many folks bite their tongues—or worse, they *don't*—when they see a family in a restaurant, all barely speaking to each other because their eyes are fixated on personal screens for the duration of the meal. At this, many shake their heads, and wonder: How did it come to be that an entire population appears to be addicted to technology, when many of us recall a day—during our own childhoods—when our homes may not have even sported a single TV or telephone? Beyond this, is anybody really at fault, and if so, does casting blame do the situation *any* good? As Lindsey Pollak's comment points out, from a Millennial point of view, the situation merely springs from the setting in which the younger generation was raised.

When it comes down to it, the age gap feeds a significant part of this matter, but the issue runs deeper: The development of the brain is affected by an overabundance of technology. For many people, mass amounts of screen time literally reroute and alter the brain's neural pathways, influencing the ability to connect emotionally and socially with others, interfering with such human attributes as empathy and relatability, and contributing to isolation, depression, and an inward focus (often interpreted by others as narcissism). Beyond this, excess digital interface diminishes the ability to feel a sense of mastery or personal competence. These are detrimental losses, because they keep a person from having the courage and self-confidence to venture into purposeful life pathways, such as pursuing academic success, overcoming personal obstacles with problem-solving and critical thinking, and even taking larger risks, such as launching entrepreneurial endeavors or stepping out on a limb to pursue a professional promotion.

Millennials are a force to be reckoned with, for certain. In fact, I believe they vastly underestimate themselves. After all, this group makes up the largest generation in history, the most numerous labor force, and the most massive group of voters. Coupling this information with the game-changing advances the world has seen over the past several decades, many feel overwhelmed by the young generation. Part of the divide between age groups is that older people were raised without such digital exposure, and thus often misread the inward focus as narcissism. While there are members of each generation who may display this personality disorder, it is usually a misconception and misappropriation of the term. When brain development has been altered to cause a personality to be more inward-focused at best—withdrawn, isolated, and lonely at worst—many times, the lack of emotional connection is more about upbringing than about an over-inflated ego.

Furthermore, this doesn't mean I'm claiming an entire generation has some sort of brain-development issue that makes them less compassionate than other age groups. In fact, that is completely false. As a whole, Millennials are some of the most benevolent, caring people on the planet. They are activists—kind, caring, generous, unconditionally accepting, and loving people who are motivated to invest in their community, thus showing an unusually high rate of generativity for their ages. These are all amazing, even biblically-endorsed attributes that, channeled in the wrong direction, can cause disaster. However, when pointed to the correct harvest, this group might be one of the strongest forces for good this world has ever seen.

THINGS HAVE REALLY CHANGED...

When I was very young, there was a single TV in my house and one rotary-dial radio. We didn't get our first telephone until I was almost four. During the day, I would usually go outside and play. There was a patio in the backyard on which stood a six-feet-wide, one-foot-deep wading pool that left enough space on the concrete for me to ride a tricycle in circles. Nearby stood a basic swing set, where I would glide back and forth through the air while singing entire albums of Christian music—by memory, beginning with the first song and resounding all the way through the last song of the LP record of artists such as Evie, Don Francisco, and even hymns I had learned in church. My mother—a stay-at-home mom at the time—was always nearby, either tending her flower garden or otherwise occupying herself within arm's reach.

After long afternoons of play in the sun, I would go inside the house, still sopping wet from my escapade in the pool, and Mom would wrap me in a towel and watch a little TV with me. We usually had to choose between the *Mickey Mouse Club* and *Gilligan's Island*. When it was raining or otherwise undesirable outside, I played indoors, dressing my dolls in clothes sewn by my mother. She also often made "homework" for me, kick-starting my education by teaching me the alphabet, basic math, spelling, phonics, and even letter-writing. I engaged in role-play games with her, such as an activity that we called "Howdy, Neighbor;" wherein I would pack a small suitcase and go outside using the back door. I would then walk around the small house to the front door and knock. When she answered the door (already knowing of course that I was on the other side), I would come in and say, "Howdy, neighbor! I came to stay with you for a few days!" We would then have make-believe conversations about our imaginary lives, families, and even careers. Often, she'd ask me if I would like to help her cook supper or with some other activity that she needed to do in real life, and I would jump in willingly, thus engaging in learning that was fun and developmentally beneficial.

My mom was my companion, my teacher, and my best friend. Later in the day, after my dad got home from work, our entire family would gather around the table to eat a home-cooked meal made from scratch by my mother. In the evening, our rotary-dial radio brought the sounds of the local Christian station into our living room, while I curled up in a blanket just before bed. This may sound like a romanticized or story-book childhood memory, but I assure you that it's an honest representation of the first four years of my life.

LEFT TO THEIR OWN DEVICES

Sadly, the childhood recalled by many of our young adults is a much different tale. For Millennials, statistics show that as few as 14 percent were cared for at home by a relative.[136] For many, daycare was an all-too-real part of the daily routine. Many factors play into this transformation. Due to mounting economic stressors, many families have been forced to transition from single to double incomes, leaving no parent at home to care for children. An increasing number of single-parent households cause the need for children to be cared for outside the home as well. Further contributing to the situation is that more individuals are seeking improved employment opportunities, so they are more willing to relocate farther away from families than many were in previous generations. This limits the ability of relatives to provide childcare while parents are working or seeking higher education.

I should state now that professional childcare is not at the root of the digital overload in our youth of today, as many who provide such care offer educational, constructive, artistic activities with opportunities for role-play with peers and other developmentally profitable undertakings. For some children, these caregivers even interact *more* with these children than their own parents can. Above and beyond this, children in some homes experience parental neglect, where the overabundance of technological exposure takes place as well. In other, less intentional situations, well-meaning parents may allow such over-indulgences, unaware of the consequences children may face as a result. Regardless of the reason, suffice it to say that over the last three decades, the amount of time spent watching TV and playing video games has dramatically increased for a majority of children. As we will discuss in upcoming pages, this vastly impacts the ability to develop a secure attachment to others, has the potential to permanently alter the chemistry of all future interpersonal relationships, changes the way the brain processes information and thinks critically, can delay or impede problem-solving skills of all types, and can even hinder the development of a healthy self-esteem.

The Importance of Attachment

Stephen Sondheim, in his famous Broadway musical *Into the Woods*, wrote the lyrics, "Careful the things you say, children will listen. Careful the things you do, children will see. And learn."[137] In the early years of childhood (from infancy through age six), caregivers make the largest impact on a child's ability to develop healthy attachments to others. Through the process of receiving care as an infant and then as a toddler, the life-long pace is set for quality interpersonal relationships. The caliber of attachment skills formed during this time likewise helps shape a sense of self and identity, along with confidence and sense of mastery. In this way, the earliest traces of attachment become the fiber by which lasting success can be made or broken. When this process isn't followed in a healthy and functional way, or if reliable, constant, and compassionate caregiving isn't available, children may suffer from anxiety, depression, insecurity, or even a withdrawn nature, setting them up to develop a negative self-image. Studies have even linked the attachment process during the earliest phases of childhood with the success of romantic relationships in adulthood, directly correlating elements such as quality of interaction, professed contentment with a relationship, and even satisfaction with co-parenting skills.[138] (This correlation often influences why people are attracted to a partner who behaves like his or her own opposite-gender parent.)

ROLE-PLAY

Role-play is an important part of early childhood development, nurturing growth in many categories: interpersonal relationships, interests, dreams, goals, concept of self, perception of self by others, social expertise, and even motor and language skills. Laura E. Berk states: "Preschoolers who spend more time engaged in socio-dramatic play are better at inhibiting impulses, regulating emotion, and taking personal responsibility for following classroom rules."[139] Many characteristics of adults can be traced back to this time when they were allowed to "try on" different roles and characters, deciding which attributes they wanted to carry with them into later chapters of life, and which ones to discard.

SCREEN TIME'S IMPACT ON ATTACHMENT

Statistics show that most children begin watching television before they turn two, and between the ages of two and five, the typical child spends thirty-two hours a week engaged in this activity.[140] Between the ages of six through eleven, the reported time spent drops to twenty-eight hours per week.[141] During these hours, 97 percent of the viewing time is spent watching live TV.[142] Beyond this, 71 percent of children between eight and eighteen years of age reportedly have a TV in their bedroom, and they likewise spend an average of 1.5 hours *more* than those who don't.[143] Those who spend the most time watching TV also often do so in isolation and without supervision or a parental filter. Furthermore, two-thirds of households report leaving television sets on while eating meals, substituting interaction with family for a digital interface.[144]

The danger this poses surfaces over time and on many levels, ranging from encouraging a sedentary lifestyle and robbing children of healthy interactive relationships to barricading their interest in engaging in constructive responsibilities such as chores or homework.

While many parents are aware that too much television has dubious side effects, a great number of them don't realize how intrusive it is to the development of a young child's brain. Spending too much time away from other people can contribute to deep-seeded feelings of loneliness and isolation, and remaining plugged in to some sort of media is no substitution for this personal interaction. While many educational TV programs purport to help children learn, experts remain consistent on the stance that we are uncertain about how viewing impacts the brain development of a person under the age of two.

Many qualified authorities go a step further, asserting that a child under the age of twenty-four months cannot—in any cognitive way—relate to or interact with movements taking place on a screen. This may seem contradictory, since very young babies often respond to a well-lit screen by smiling, reaching, or excitedly flailing arms and legs. But experts say that before at least the age of two (and older for some children), toddlers, while fascinated by the lights and colors of the media, are not yet able to translate what they observe through this format into *real-life scenarios.*

For example, a series of studies conducted in the late 1990s and early 2000s included two-year-old children being shown, on a live feed, a person hiding an object in an adjoining room. Others of the same age group observed the actions through an open window into the area. When taken into the room and asked to retrieve the object, those who had observed in person readily recovered the object they had seen being hidden. Those who had watched via screen were either unable to or had difficulty in completing this task.[145] This inability to relate activity taking place through media to the real world is called the "video deficit effect," which is the product of a lack of personal interaction between people on the part of the young viewer. Many baby/toddler educational programs have attempted to counteract this by asking questions, pausing to allow time for the child to answer, then responding with replies such as, "That's right!" This, however, does not guarantee that a little one is cognitively interacting with what he or she sees taking place, and as said before, many experts still maintain that while children may be *entertained* by the colors or shapes they are observing, they don't experience any *healthy interaction.*

If this type of activity continues for long periods, the risk becomes mounting isolation and loneliness, the likes of which may be similar to putting a person in a room for hours on end with no one or nothing to interact with beyond an object portraying moving light. The equivalent for an adult could be isolation for extended times with only a lava lamp or disco ball to break the monotony. Considering that this could be a very young child's activity for as many as thirty-two hours a week, this deters the ability to attach to other people.

THOUGHT WELLS

The phrase "thought wells" as used here refers to the concept of a person's ability to ponder a particular concept, similar to a "train of thought," but specifically referring to the amount of time and depth that he or she is able to dedicate to that particular line of meditation. It should be expressed, however, that the "depth" of a thought well is not indicative of an individual's depth as a person, but rather to his or her ability to devote time and energy to a particular idea. For example, a person thinking heavily and deeply along one train of thought at a given moment experiences a deep thought well, while another who is multitasking with divided attention utilizes multiple, shallower thought wells.

Furthermore, thought wells are affected by the continual interruption of cognitive flow caused by television programming, and this creates another means by which generations are divided. For the person who watches a lot of TV, a typical scenario is a half-hour to one-hour plot (episode) typically divided into fifteen-minute segments between which two to four commercials are inserted. This pattern pulls the mind in and out of the primary storyline, while focus is disturbed by several smaller intrusions wherein decisions or urges to make purchases are introduced, after which the original content is reintroduced for another quarter of an hour. Then, the cycle repeats. In contrast, people who prefer to read a novel (such as many from the older generations) can submerge themselves into an uninterrupted thought path until *they, themselves* choose to bookmark the page and disengage.

When the type of unsolicited distraction we're accustomed to when viewing television becomes habitual, it changes our thought processing. Thought wells become shallower and more easily abandoned, but we have become acclimated to taking on *a greater number* of them. The long-term differences, in regard to interactions with *people*, manifests as follows: members of one age group are entertaining several narrower trains of thought at the same time, and are thus more skilled at multi-tasking, while those in another age group are inclined to ponder a particular thought well with more depth and whole-hearted focus over a greater length of time. The friction comes in when those in the latter group become frustrated with what appears to be a younger generation of people who can't seem to sit still or give serious consideration to the profound, solemn elements of life. The younger people are equally agitated with what they deem as unjustified, age-related judgment of their busy lifestyles in a world that has changed and demands a fast pace.

As children age beyond toddlerhood, the hours spent watching TV begin to diversify to include video games, social media, Internet, and handheld devices. Addictions to such activities often begin to form within this age range, when the child's brain begins to filter media differently. The inability of a toddler (before age two or two and a half years) to transfer events from the television into their perception of reality then alters. What previously held no real-world relevance to the child begins to seem very real, and the ability to distinguish events viewed in media from those occurring in real life diminishes. In short, the child is now subconsciously unable to separate happenings on screen from those in real life; when he or she witnesses something on television, it now has the potential to seem every bit as real as watching it take place in person.

Think about the implications of this: Children become cognitively unable to effectively compartmentalize acts of violence, war, racism, sexual assault, or other heinous activity into the "fictitious" category of the brain. Witnessing such an event on television has the capacity to impact them as though it happened in their living room—*right in front of them.* Because role-play is so pertinent to a child's development, it is common for the acts they've seen on TV to find their way into early imitative play—regardless of whether the action was good or bad.[146] What we adults take for granted as mere entertainment thus impacts our children as though they have witnessed the real event, and then conditions them to then re-enact it.

Neural Atrophy and Brain Development Interference

Worse than this, between the ages of two and six, the brain finishes most of its physical development, reaching 90 percent of its adult capacity.[147] During this time, and particularly between the ages of four and five, a process called "synaptic pruning" takes place. This is when "neurons that are seldom stimulated lose their connective fibers, and the number of synapses gradually declines."[148] This is the process by which the brain selects which neural connectors to fine-tune and which ones to slowly phase out. Neural connections within the brain that are not being stimulated are at risk of atrophy. See what Dr. Victoria Dunckley of the American Board or Psychiatry and Neurology, the American Academy of Child and Adolescent Psychiatry, and the American Board of Integrative Holistic Medicine (to name only a few of her qualifications) has to say on this:

Multiple studies have shown atrophy (shrinkage or loss of tissue volume) in gray matter areas (where "processing" occurs) in internet/gaming addiction. Areas affected included the important frontal lobe, which governs executive functions, such as planning...prioritizing, organizing, and impulse control.... Volume loss was also seen in the striatum, which is involved in reward pathways and the suppression of socially unacceptable impulses. A finding of particular concern was damage to an area known as the insula, which is involved in our capacity to develop empathy and compassion for others and our ability to integrate physical signals with emotion. Aside from the obvious link to violent behavior, these skills dictate the depth and quality of personal relationships.[149]

Dunckley also explains that dopamine, sometimes referred to as the "feel-good hormone,"[150] is released during video-gaming activity, which feeds addiction to such activities, particularly in teenage boys, by creating "craving or urges for gaming [that] produces brain changes that are similar to drug cravings."[151] A large percentage of damage that takes place due to too much screen exposure is inflicted upon the frontal lobe, interfering with its development throughout the adolescent years and well into the mid twenties. "Frontal lobe development, in turn, largely determines success in every area of life—from sense of well-being to academic or career success to relationship skills."[152]

Since the brain adapts during development phases during childhood, ability to process emotion, thoughts, and skills are constructed simultaneously. The brain revises its patterns based on two types of incoming criteria: experience-expectant brain growth, wherein ordinary activities that happen organically teach the young mind; and experience-dependent brain growth, which shapes thought and learning capabilities using intentional learning experiences that vary between individuals, environments, and even cultures.[153] An example of experience-expectant growth would be skills such as learning to walk or eat with a fork, while experience-dependent growth renders specific skills and abilities, such as playing a sport, dancing, or learning to play a musical instrument. For example, the brain of a violinist differs from that of a poet, because each one has honed specific skills within different regions of the brain over an extended period.[154]

Too much exposure to screens leaves children spending hours in isolation and intense loneliness, away from attachment to people, and hinders the ability to develop emotions like empathy while often fostering reenactments of violent scenes. Then, as the screen fixation spreads out to include more addictive activities such as playing video games, that behavior adapts to violence while other neural connections run the risk of atrophy. Meanwhile, many experience the release of dopamine, rewarding and reinforcing such behavior within the brain. In addition, these learned behaviors influence real-life relationship skills and affect the ability to find success in all areas of life. This severely impacts all processes of attachment throughout young adulthood with repercussions that last throughout life.

EMERGENCE OF THE GAMING DISORDER

While the World Health Organization hasn't yet classified an official screen-addiction epidemic yet, it recognizes "Gaming Disorder" in the upcoming *International Classification of Diseases* due to its addictive nature and correlated behaviors.[155]

Pediatric experts assert that young children—especially under the age of two—must learn using all five senses, thus screen time—during which all five senses are NOT engaged—is detrimental to development. Parents of children within this age group are encouraged to allow no television time for their toddlers. The Parents as Teachers National

Center encourages caregivers to give children a setting wherein they can "explore, move, manipulate, smell, touch, and repeat as they learn,"[156] and links too much electronic media exposure to "attention difficulties…delays in language…develop[ment of] smaller vocabularies… more violent and aggressive play and behavior…and…[obesity]."[157] Beyond this, there seems to be no strong argument (other than parental convenience) that large amounts of time spent watching television or video gaming is beneficial or even harmless. It doesn't appear that these activities in any way foster stronger cognitive development, better social skills, increased attention span, or enhanced interpersonal interaction. Yet, the average child over five spends approximately seven hours a day engaging in these very activities.

In addition, the American Psychological Association reports that those watching mainstream TV programming are exposed to as many as twenty acts of violence every hour, while other statistics reveal that the average child in America will see up to twelve thousand acts of violence each year through this activity.[158] Furthermore, both the Parents as Teachers National Center and the American Psychological Association fortify a statement made previously: Because role-play is an essential part of childhood development, those who witness violence regularly are more likely to reenact these events toward others, while simultaneously struggling to develop compassion toward the victim.[159]

EMOTIONAL DISCONNECT

Perhaps most alarming of everything said so far regarding digital interaction's influence upon children is the fact that extensive periods of screen time decrease a developing child's ability to procure emotions such as empathy, and that this diminishes the quality of interpersonal relationships that child will experience throughout life. Unfortunately, a 2017 study released by the General Social Survey reported that the "number of Americans with no close friends has tripled since 1985."[160] Nearly 25 percent of those questioned in this survey reported having zero confidantes. Unfortunately, this epidemic is cyclical: People who are lonely tend to withdraw, further feeding seclusion within themselves, while simultaneously becoming more unavailable to those around them who in turn may also be solitary.

It has been stated at a previous point in this book that Millennials are called, amongst other names, the loneliest generation, and there's no debate that they suffer from chronic isolation. Taking this into context with the information given earlier in this book regarding the anxiety and suicide rates, addiction epidemics, and the way the modern world has shaped the mind of young people through media, identity politics, and other adversities, it becomes apparent that we are not dealing with a generation of "monsters," as some have painted them to be. On the contrary, we have an entire populace of individuals who have been dealt an unfair hand and are likely scrambling to adapt. Our older generation, zealous to help but often unsure of what tactic to adopt, often become exasperated by the situation and, sadly, our youth become the object of the outrage. But if each age group could foster a new perspective, we could meet in the middle and possibly reach this generation of lonely, isolated individuals who need the opportunity to experience love and hope.

When observing some of the trends followed by young adults of today from a new standpoint, we can see clues that they often use their own means, particular to their generation, of trying to connect with the world around them. Regardless of whether they have established good skills at interacting, many try. Consider the hours spent by the masses on such websites as Facebook, Twitter, Pinterest, LinkedIn, Instagram, Tumblr, and myriad other social media outlets. This means of connecting has become a widespread tool that many use to try to form lasting relationships with others and relieve the loneliness epidemic that plagues our modern youth. Where previous generations had community activities to bring people together—book clubs, neighborhood barbecues, block parties—the modern age has brought in digital hosts for such interaction. And this stands to reason, as this very interface has become the means through which so many common activities are conducted: bill paying, shopping, schooling, and so much more are now carried out online. Naturally, the social aspect of life has followed suit.

Let's digress for just a moment to discuss childhood development again, this time referring to Lev Vygotsky (1896–1934), a developmental psychologist who introduced and developed monumentally vital contributions to the modern scientific study of childhood development. Within the realms of early psychological expansion, Vygotsky claimed that it is vital to provide children with opportunities to play in ways that are culturally meaningful and interactive. He explained that within the realms of make-believe, engagement in play with caregivers and people of other mentor-type roles, a child develops stronger elements of identity and self-esteem, which foster healthier interactions and endeavors throughout the entire lifespan. Findings support that a stimulating environment, while helpful, is not enough—in and of itself—to encourage healthy social development. In a nutshell: We can place a young child in a room filled with educational, artistic, and entertaining toys, but these objects' potential to contribute to cognitive development are limited when there is no mentor or peer with whom the child can enjoy such resources.

SOCIAL MEDIA: MORE HURT THAN HELP

Social media is not a fulfilling substitution for real-life interaction; thus, instead of helping with the modern issue of chronic loneliness, it worsens the problem. For one thing, it seems to be a chronic habit of the social media user to compare profiles and life-events of others with his or her own. This comparison game is a slippery slope, and many experts link it to further anxiety or depression. Many who feel lonely turn to social media to connect with others, but this has destructive consequences, since most people don't post a realistic snapshot of their own circumstances. Often, profiles seem to be polarized between two extremes: those who chronically post depressive or lonely comments (likely in the hopes that others will send them love, encouragement, or attention) and others who exaggerate the joy and success of their daily lives (often causing further depression and loneliness in others, who feel their own lives don't measure up). As a result, social media users easily develop a skewed concept of "normal."

Perhaps that is where the Millennial label "the most perfectionist generation" comes in. "A new study finds that this generation carries much higher levels of perfectionism, and that these elevated expectations may be to blame [for their high levels of depression, anxiety, and suicidal thoughts]."[161] Often, this generation is chided for its propensity to have high expectations, but those poking fun rarely see the ramifications of such an attitude. Since these individuals have higher aspirations than the rest of the world often holds, they're often the *victims* of their own lofty hopes. In essence, when their high standards aren't met, they're disappointed. Even worse, because they derive much of their hope from the images they see of peers touting (exaggerated?) accomplishments, they often view themselves as failures. Furthermore, they operate under the false impression that they're the *only ones* experiencing this letdown. The result is escalated sense of loss and depression.

Experts say that perfectionism is divided into three typical categories: 1) "self–oriented perfectionism,"[162] which is self-inflicted pressure to reach unrealistically high aspirations; 2) "socially prescribed perfectionism,"[163] pressure from others to reach excessively high standards, often combined with criticism at failure; and 3) "other-oriented perfectionism,"[164] which is emphasis placed on others to attain unreasonably extraordinary achievements. In a recent survey, Millennials scored higher than previous generations in all three categories of perfectionism. Furthermore, authorities linked social media to this condition, explaining that "seeing peers portrayed with perfect bodies, achieving noteworthy goals, or modeling RomCom ["romantic-comedy"]-worthy relationships, increases feelings of insecurity"[165] and thus feeds the sense of personal failure already fostered by the comparison game that is fueled by social media.

Furthermore, interpersonal connections made online are rarely satisfying and deep, and are usually short-lived, superficial, or sometimes even in some way predatory. When these attempts at subsidizing human interaction are ill-met, the chronic loneliness experienced by an individual worsens, and destructive behavior such as addiction and depression rises. Because seclusion feeds depression, and depression leads to other issues such as lack of motivation and success in personal and professional areas, it indirectly hinders a variety of accomplishments. The response to such circumstances often is to withdraw, creating further isolation. When people feel as though they have nothing to offer the world in terms of personal or professional success and they feel detached from interactive relationships, the issue perpetuates and the problem only worsens. A vast majority of our young adults spent more time during their formative years (early childhood) with media than in a setting where they were able to enjoy quality exchanges with caregivers and peers. As a result, many have suffered an interrupted attachment development. The result of this chronic loneliness is to further withdraw.

IS THIS REALLY REALITY?

Another popular means of connecting with the outside world manifests through the raging trend of reality TV, which is usually portrays *anything but* reality. However, it provides a way for a solitary person to peek into someone else's life and feel some association with that individual. For those who don't know how to break out of isolation, this type of interface seems to add excitement and the opportunity to experience human interaction, but without the discomfort of having to risk personal rejection or conflict.

What a deal, right?

One problem: All the negative side-effects of social media are often the wreckage of this genre of media as well. The yearning for meaningful friendship with others still exists. On the surface, reality TV seems to meet these needs, because, for all practical purposes, social activities have been observed and curiosities have been satisfied. Yet this leaves those who can't identify the source of their desires (love and friendship interaction) feeling a deeper sense of emptiness they cannot seem to vocalize. For those whose ability to interact/attach with others was interrupted early on by overabundance of media, the very nuance of such a concept can be nearly or completely impossible to put into words. This heightens the sense of failure and isolation, while the feeling that the situation is hopeless swells due to the inability to put a finger on the problem. In turn, self-esteem and identity, as they pertain to the concept of one's role in the family and community, are negatively affected.

COMMERCIAL COMPONENT

One of the most frequent complaints about Millennials is that they're "overly opinionated." This may be partially true, and it can be a language barrier between generations (more on this later). As for the suggestion that these individuals are opinionated, there may be a justifiable cause. Let's take a minute to explore this.

Perhaps you've seen the movie *A Christmas Story*, wherein nine-year-old Ralphie Parker wants more than anything else in the world to receive a Red Ryder Range 200 Shot BB gun. In one scene, Ralphie had saved up a required number of proofs of purchase to obtain a membership in the Little Orphan Annie Secret Circle. After waiting weeks for the initiation package to arrive in the mail, the coveted parcel finally makes its appearance, wherein the boy discovers a Secret Orphan Annie Decoder. Ralphie listens intently to the radio as the announcer gives the secret code—decipherable *only* to those within Annie's Secret Circle. Suspense mounts as the young man frantically writes down the mysterious series of numbers for subsequent decrypting.

After reading the code, the announcer reminds the audience, once again, that the hidden message is confidential—only to be spoken between those who own the decoder. Ralphie races up the stairs and locks himself in the bathroom, seeking privacy while he decodes the vital message. One letter at a time, he painstakingly uncovers the message. The tension mounts as the youth begins to see the first words of the message form:

"*Be sure to…*

"Be sure to *what?*"[166] he asks frantically.

The deciphering process continues as he surmises such lofty concepts as the possibility that the fate of even the entire planet may hinge on his impending discovery. The pressure of the scene intensifies until the final words of the message are finally revealed:

"*…drink your Ovaltine.*"[167]

A moment of stunned silence follows.

"Ovaltine?" Ralphie looks up, staring bewilderedly into midair. "A crummy commercial?"[168] The boy emerges from the room older, wiser, cynical, and even jaded.

Sometimes, when I consider the Millennial generation, I'm reminded of this scene. I imagine a crowd of young adults, years removed from the ability to fall for such a trick of advertising. In fact, our youth have seen more ads than any member of the older generations. CBS News recently released a story stating that the average person now sees approximately five thousand ads each day. This is up ten times over the average five hundred ads per day the average person saw during the 1970s.[169]

This is a great example of an aspect of society that has influenced the thought development of the young person and an older person differently. Recall that, earlier in the book, I mentioned that a youth can have several thoughts of narrower capacity active at the same time, while an older person thoroughly considers one matter before moving on to the next. With the constant barrage of commercial advertising, the ability to make extremely quick decisions has, for many young people, become a habit. Thus, the decisive, independent, opinion-forming part of their thought process is much more fully developed than that of previous generations.

While engaging in one train of thought, advertisements creeping into a young person's peripheral senses can pose a mental "check yes or no" box, to which he or she is usually able to respond without missing a beat while remaining undistracted in a completely different conversation or train of thought. This is a testament to the Millennials' ability to multitask. Sounds like a great deal, right? The trade-off is that young adults often consider their predecessors as opinionated or sometimes even arrogant. The friction between age brackets manifests as follows: an older person, when sharing an opinion, may begin with contributing factors pertinent to the matter at hand, conversationally building a case until finally arriving at the stated position, having carefully relayed the facts that led to this conclusion. In contrast, many young people prefer a dialogue that moves quickly, often abruptly skimming over complexities and "cutting to the chase."

DIGITAL INFLUENCE: HERE TO STAY

Technology—for better or for worse—is here to stay. Young people, having both the benefit of and the detriment of being raised in its influence, have largely managed to adapt while older generations strive to keep up. However, the price of digital technology's prevalence within society has come at the cost of interpersonal connections, and this is still an innate human need. This said, it is vital that, as we strive to reunite age groups, we look for common ground to retain the part of technology that is useful and learn to help each other find ways to overcome technology's hindrance to human connections.

THE "LIVE-WITH-PARENTS" GENERATION

NOT YOUR GRANDPA'S GENERATION GAP

AS ALREADY STRESSED, the generation gap plays an enormous role in the tension between age groups. This is particularly due to the changes in the world over the past several decades. We've discussed how philosophical and religious evolution of thought has come to a head in the modern populace's thinking. We have also discussed how the very concept of identity has become skewed, robbing our young people of the opportunity to truly assess and chase personal legacy. Additionally, we've covered the long-term ramifications of digital technology's presence in the lives and mental development of this generation. You'd think all this would be quite enough to make a case for why Millennials are so dramatically different socially, religiously, and culturally than the older generations. Certainly, they account for an exaggerated wedge.

However, as an added factor, we must consider the economic stressors that have influenced how our current young adults navigate their lives. After all, Millennials have certainly taken a verbal bashing for the large percentages of them who live at home with parents until much older ages than that of previous generations. Yet, to young adults who are just beginning their financial life endeavors, the current circumstances play a huge role in precisely why many wait until they're older to move into their own house or apartment. These considerations, like so many others, require a shift of perspective in order to understand exactly where they're coming from when they conduct their business the way they do.

ECONOMIC ELEMENTS

Experts say that between 2000 and 2009, America withstood the worst financial crisis it had ever seen. All things considered, the amount of money lost overall far surpassed the loss that kicked off the Great Depression (although to the individual citizens who endured the Great Depression, the aftermath, in many ways, was much more challenging than that of the early 2000s). Consider what Noah Smith of *Bloomberg News* had to say in 2015 regarding the economic events that unfolded during this span:

> In 2000 the tech bubble popped, and in 2008 the housing bubble followed. Each of these asset price crashes represented $6.2 trillion dollars of financial wealth vanishing into thin air. That means each was larger, as a percentage of U.S. gross domestic product, than the stock market crash that touched off the Great Depression. In the space of a decade, we had the two biggest financial crashes in U.S. history.[170]

As the job market slowly recovered from the political and economic fallout of the years 2000–2001, "real median household income never came back to its peak in the late 1990s."[171] Worse, by the time the housing crash had taken place in 2008, the recession that followed brought repercussions that dwarfed those of the earlier 2000s. The U.S. Gross

Domestic Product (GDP) plummeted by 3.9 percent,[172] average household wealth decreased by half, and wages dropped significantly. Inflation counterweighed remaining higher-paying jobs, causing those fortunate few who were able to maintain preferable employment to struggle in an attempt to make dollars go as far as they had previously.

During this time, unemployment rose to over 10 percent (some reporting numbers as high as 19 percent[173]), causing fewer dollars to be circulated into an already-failing economy, and fewer taxes paid due to fewer wage earners caused government programs designed to stabilize such matters to likewise falter. "At the same time, of course, rapid growth in developing countries and dwindling supplies of crude oil pushed commodity prices to levels they hadn't touched in decades. Gasoline went from a little more than $1 a gallon at the start of the decade to $4."[174] This type of hyperinflation caused further financial struggle for many already wavering families.

IMPACT OF THE HOUSING CRASH

When the housing market crashed in 2008, the brunt of the economic crisis was absorbed by members of the Baby Boom and Gen X, while the oldest Millennials now in their mid-twenties were likewise directly impacted. Over time, the aftermath rippled out to remaining Millennials and Post-Millennials as well. The nature and cause of the crash in 2008 is multifaceted and complicated, and for this reason cannot be fully covered in this book. However, the situation can be summed up like this:

In previous years, banks had been discriminating in their home-mortgage lending practices. Collateral, large down payments, or other guarantees were secured before loans were advanced. When government-subsidized mortgage companies such as Fannie Mae and Freddie Mac began to buy out balances on currently existing mortgage loans from smaller, private banks, lending protocol loosened and financing became easier to obtain, making home purchases more easily available to the average consumer. A combination of issues culminated to contribute to the subsequent crash. Many who had not adequately primed for the financial ramifications of homeownership found themselves unprepared, and they soon defaulted on payments. Additionally, because of the surge in availability of easily-obtained mortgage loans, housing prices skyrocketed, and many individuals purchased homes that ordinarily would have been outside their price range (often purchased at overinflated prices). On top of this, when unemployment rates began to rise, many others were unable to sustain the high loan payments they had signed on for.

As foreclosure rates began to increase, financial institutions overcorrected by requiring more stringent paperwork for refinancing than had been demanded for the initial loans, and people who previously qualified for higher-balance financing or those whose employment was nontraditional (such as self-employed business owners or independent contractors) lost their homes when they were unable to sustain their current debt or refinance for more reasonable payments. Home-equity lines of credit further fed an already leaping flame, as homeowners either used these assets to sustain living expenses during times of unemployment or racked up balances to remodel or improve homes to maintain high market values on properties whose assessed prices were beginning to sink. Adjustable mortgage rates were a final nail in the coffin of the housing market's glory days.

Many other economic and political elements played into the powder keg that resulted in the housing crash of 2008, but as mentioned earlier, they cannot begin to be covered in this book. Suffice it to say, when Fanny Mae, Freddie Mac, and other mammoth financial institutions went belly-up in 2008, foreclosures became the epidemic that displaced millions of families and caused nearly eight million properties to be reclaimed by banks. Additionally, this crisis added more than $400 billion to the national debt.

REPERCUSSIONS OF THE RECESSION

During the housing crash and recession of 2008–2009, America's Millennial generation, the oldest of whom were born in 1981, were hitting their mid- to late- 20s. Many were graduating from college, attempting to purchase their first homes, starting families, or beginning their careers. When the economy took a nosedive and foreclosures sprung up across the countryside, many recoiled and re-strategized their plans. Additionally, many who fell victim to the economic fallout and whose lives were permanently, financially derailed during this time were themselves members of the Millennial generation. For those who were too young to be directly impacted, their parents absorbed this blow. Being eyewitness to such struggles left a strong impression on these young people, and similarly imprinted mistrust for institutions into them as well. Meghan Foley of the *Cheat Sheet* reports: "The recession caused many Americans born roughly between 1981 and 1996 to defer major adult milestones like purchasing a home or car purchases and delaying marriage."[175]

Kurt Daniel of *Investopedia Insights* sheds further light on this matter: "Just when college grads thought they'd be starting their careers and laying the foundation for their eventual retirements, the [economic] crisis pulled the rug out from under their feet.... It didn't help that those graduates left school with a pile of student loans the size of which their parents' generation never had to confront."[176] When it comes to those seeking to enter the employment market after the recession of 2008, experts claim that Millennials, especially those between the ages of twenty-five and thirty-four, have been hit the hardest of any age bracket.[177] It is also said that despite the economy's slow but steady gain, "the current recovery has not spread to younger workers as previous recoveries did."[178] While this may seem contradictory, since Millennials are said to make up the largest age group in the current workforce, it must also be noted that 48 percent of the unemployed population also falls within this age bracket.[179] Unfortunately, "Millennials will not be unable to make up this ground, because early adulthood is when productivity is greatest and pay raises more significant. A depressed starting salary means a worker will likely earn much less for the rest of his or her career."[180] Additionally, while the post-recession economy claims to have recreated the nearly nine million jobs lost during the recession, the newly introduced jobs are of lower quality than those previously offered. Many companies have reduced costs by replacing higher-paying, prestigious jobs offering superior benefits with minimum-wage or entry-level positions offering fewer benefits.[181]

The strain on the economy caused by the recession of 2008–2009 landed on all age groups, including older individuals (those over the age of fifty-five), who continue to work in the labor force rather than retiring as previous generations may have. For this reason, a significant number of job openings have been delayed, and many are managerial or supervisory positions that younger people eye with envy. This results in workplace friction that will be covered a little later in this chapter.

This is the financial climate our Millennials faced when they came of age. For those who were still children or teens at the time, many recall with vivid memory the struggle they watched their parents undergo. For a large percentage of this age group, recollections of a jobless, struggling parent facing foreclosure paints the picture of what they believe their own future to be: one of imminent, looming failure in an economy that has set the average laborers up for defeat despite their best efforts.

In addition, inflation continues to increase, making living on entry-level wages nearly impossible. Likewise, when young adults decide to move into their own living quarters, lease agreements often require exorbitant down payments and deposits with lengthy terms rather than month-to-month allowances—another element that contributes to delay in moving away from parents' homes. Many members of older generations tease young people who opt to remain in their parents' home into their twenties and even thirties—even accusing them of being lazy, which may occasionally be the case, but laziness certainly does not describe *all* of those within this age bracket who remain at home. Taking into account the financial defeat many young adults are certain they face (even if their situation isn't as bad as they perceive), it is reasonable to accept that many other, more complicated, dynamics factor into this hesitancy.

Sadly, many economists also state that young adults will likely never own or invest in real estate: "The number of young Americans choosing to buy a home has significantly declined since the housing market collapse. The data suggests that Millennials not only have less saved for a down payment, but they also are less likely to see the real estate market as a safe bet."[182] Furthermore, an Urban Institute analysis of the housing market as it pertains to the Millennial generation reported: "Baby Boomers and Gen Xers saw homeownership as a place to live and as a store of value and the best way to build wealth, but millennials, whose formative years occurred during the Great Recession, are unlikely to take the wealth-building assumption as a given."[183]

Another factor that plays into our younger population's economic standing is their general aversion to financial risk. This is a direct result of either witnessing their parents' struggles or experiencing them as young adults in the early 2000s. This causes them to be more conservative with investments, slowing the building of wealth for those who have the capital to invest in the first place. Experts cite "evidence that younger Americans who do put money into 410(k)s are opting for a more conservative approach that offers little opportunity for long-term growth. A Bankrate survey found that 30% of adults ages 18 to 37 believe cash is the best investment choice for money they won't need [as opposed to other, higher-yielding investments] for at least 10 years."[184] What all of this means for the long-term: Even the most disciplined, financially strategizing Millennials face lower financial gains throughout their adult lives, impacting large-scale investment economics and personal wealth-building accruals. Sadly, in general, the stock- and real estate- markets have become distrusted investments by our younger adults, and investments with higher-percentage yields (due to their greater risk factors) have been declined in lieu of safer, lower-yielding ventures. For others, building a savings account is a dream that many aren't sure will *ever* be realized.

FRICTION IN THE WORKPLACE

THE STUDENT DEBT CRISIS

At the beginning of the 2018 school year, CNBC released a story stating that "average [student] debt at [college or university] graduation is currently around $30,000, up from $10,000 in the early 1990s,"[185] while the overall remaining student debt is expected to reach $2 trillion by 2022.[186] Beyond this, experts say that much of this will remain unpaid, as many graduates have fallen into a state of default due to payments that can soar as high as nearly $1,000 per month. Payments of this magnitude, combined with the aftermath of the housing crisis of 2008, create doubt that many members of the young generation will ever own their own home, as previously stated. For many, the memories of a shaky economy claiming their childhood home out from under financially-struggling parents leave a deeply resonating impression.

It has already been stated that for these folks, purchasing a home is often not deemed a safe investment. Additionally, as we have said, many watched their parents struggle with layoffs and unemployment during the early 2000s. Thus, many young adults have opted to invest not in real estate, stocks, or other such ventures, but in *their own careers*, seeing this as a worthier investment. After all, knowledge cannot be taken away, foreclosed upon, or repossessed. On the other hand, it *can* be transferred from one setting to another, unlike real estate or other material investments, only to find some circumstance outside their own control has somehow subverted the asset. Many people refer to material wealth by stating: "You can't take it with you."[187] For young adults of today, it seems that maybe they have found the *one* loophole to this rule.

Furthermore, the additional job security that comes with a degree, coupled with promises of higher-paying employment, make convincing arguments as to why finances should be invested in continuing education rather than in property or other seemingly vulnerable ventures. The result is a segment of the population who remain at their parents' homes while they're continuing their education. Many older folks struggle to understand why such a great number of young adults are still "living in their parents' basement." But considering the economic climate of Millennials' childhood and early adulthood, it is easy to understand why many have been studiously pursuing bachelor's and master's degrees.

Unfortunately, this is likewise not an ideal scenario. State funding cuts in education subsidization equaling $9 billion between 2008 and 2017[188] contributed to skyrocketing tuition prices that students were forced to offset with additional debt, and the average expenditure on continued education per year is now $30,000 per student per year.[189] In light of this climbing student debt, the question asked by many in the older generations(a great number of whom managed to achieve success without the benefit of secondary education) becomes: Why would anyone continue his or her education while watching these numbers pile up? When the debt reaches a level that no longer seems manageable, why continue to pursue additional degrees? The answer is that, for many, it has become a trap that they only know to continue. Allow me to explain.

Many of these individuals, somewhere near the end of their primary educational years, were sold a package: The path to success is to graduate high school, attend college or a university, obtain a degree, and then pursue a successful—and likewise secure and high-paying—career. Many well-meaning parents encouraged this plan, recalling their own financial struggles of previous years. Young and old alike, for the most part, agreed: Secondary education is the key to avoiding the kind of financial difficulties navigated by older generations. It was like a fairy tale. Many young adults bought it, literally, utilizing *borrowed* dollars. While it is not always the case, some schools are even predatory about how they represent their tuition amounts and other costs. Often, proposed future salaries are exaggerated to prospective students, not truly representing the *entry level* income of a particular line of work, instead projecting an *advanced* salary.

I returned to school a few years back, and will never forget one school I was inquiring about. I called to find out how much tuition and other costs would be, and the woman on the other end of the line said told me to get a pencil and a piece of paper. I did as she requested. She continued, "Now I want you to draw a vertical line down the center of the page, creating two columns. At the top of the left column, I want you to write, 'financial aid's responsibility.' Over the column on the right, I want you to write, 'my responsibility.'"

Suspicious, I followed her request. I was beginning to feel as though she were dodging my question. She began by giving me a tuition price per semester, which I was told to write in the column on the left. Then, a price for books was added under "financial aid's responsibility" as well. She continued to outline many expenses related to attending this college, assigning the bulk of them to the list on the left side. When her recitation was completed, I noticed that the "my responsibility" column showed less than $300 worth of expenses, posting only application fees and a few other miscellaneous costs, while most of the total fell under "financial aid's responsibility." The left side of the page was loaded with tens of thousands of dollars' in costs.

"I'm confused," I remember saying. "I need to know how much, *out-of-pocket*, my education is going to cost me. Isn't financial aid just a loan?"

She answered in the affirmative. I continued, "Then this is *all* my responsibility eventually, right? So why are there two columns? I don't understand." I was frustrated with the notion that while I was making a huge financial decision that would impact my entire future, I had the sneaking feeling that she was not being forthcoming.

"Well, not until you graduate," was her simple answer. I ended the call and checked that school off my list of prospective colleges. Unfortunately, for many who have never had to navigate financial waters, this simple "two-list" trick would have been enough to coerce students into thinking their debt isn't their own financial responsibility or that they could "just pay later, after they graduate," at which time, they might assume that their expected, inflated salary would easily provide for such payments.

Please note that I am *in no way* stating that secondary education is not worthwhile; in fact, I am a student myself and love nearly every minute of it (except finals week!). Likewise, in our current economy, those who don't have degrees often struggle to find jobs offering adequate wages for survival. Often, older folks have trouble grasping why college is so important to a young adult when they themselves were forced to work without such benefits; however, many fail to take into account that the nature of employment has certainly changed over the decades.

With the outsourcing of factories and production companies, more positions within the US these days are of a technical nature, and increasing numbers of companies require a degree for coveted positions. The concern surrounding secondary education comes into play when considering the huge amount of debt accrued while pursuing a degree. Furthermore, when this debt is downplayed or future earnings are over-inflated to a prospective student—thus having their entire financial future misrepresented—it is the young adult who pays a long-term price for this dishonesty.

Beyond this, another issue complicates matters for a person who acquires student loans. When these loans are taken out, they are placed in deferred status, meaning that payments are not required until after graduation or a break in schooling that lasts longer than six months. At that point, payments on the balance become due, regardless of whether the borrower received a degree or merely stopped attending school. For some student loans, interest is subsidized by the government until payments are required; for others, interest accrues for the entire life of the loan.

Many students feel a sense of urgency to pursue higher levels of education (thus taking on additional debt) until they have a degree that allows them to get a job that pays enough to offset the amount of loan payments that are now due. If they stop attending school or drop below part-time status, they are held responsible to begin paying off these loans. At the associate degree, entry-level employment market, most jobs pay somewhat more than regular, non-degreed jobs, and additionally, new fields requiring expertise (and thus not available to those with no degree) open up. Salaries and opportunity rise again at the bachelor's degree level, and again at master's and doctorate stages. But as the person pursues those additional heights of education, the mounting debt likewise rises, offsetting the increasing salary the student hopes for.

In the meantime, as more individuals follow this strategy, obtaining additional degrees, the employment market is further flooded with highly qualified individuals—other, newly graduated university/college students—all looking for the few existing, well-paying jobs with good benefits.

An Absurd, But Realistic, Comparison

When graduates start looking for jobs directly after college, many times they're hoping to find a dream job. As stated earlier, for many, their education was sold to them with the promise of being the key to a high-paying, prestigious position. Secondary education, for many, is followed on the premise that if they study hard and are willing to take on some student debt, they will be rewarded with a financially secure future. In light of this, it is understandable how, the more studens have invested in continued education—thus in the dream of a worthwhile career—the more frustrated they may feel when entering the workforce only to see that many others are also in line for the same jobs, promotions, or management positions. For many, this generates a defeated feeling of having been the brunt of a costly and cruel joke. At the very least, for many, this disillusionment seems unfair.

Many vocal individuals have been publicly off-put by Millennial's "unrealistically high expectations"[190] upon entering the workforce. But understanding the young adult's position can make members of the older generation sympathetic. To the younger people, they have "arrived"—taken on the debt, studied, and opted for education over the pursuit of marriage, children, or even living independently. Now, after years of this self-sacrifice and monetary investment, they have graduated, obtained a degree, and found employment in a field of choice. A young adult in this position is thrilled to finally enter the professional scene, expecting to collect on a vastly expensive investment. Recall that these individuals were sold an idea of a career—one that they *financed.* Unlike the members of previous generations whose primary investments were seeded elsewhere, this is how many young adults chose to invest their assets.

Now, as many of these young people enter the employment scene, it's natural for them to want to collect on their investment. A comparable scenario for an older person might be as follows: Imagine that after saving for years, you've finally chosen and made a down payment on an expensive home. You've signed the paperwork for the financing, made the first loan installment, and finished all necessary business at the title company. When it is time to collect the keys and take possession of your investment, you find that several other people are in line for the keys to the property as well. Worse, you're told that others have signed similar documents and obtained similar financing, and *only some* of the people present will be given access to the real estate in question. Make no mistake: You will be held liable for all agreed-upon payments, but you *may or may not be given ownership* of your purchase. Your attitude may shift dramatically—as I know mine would.

You might say something like, "Wait a minute here—I *financed* this purchase. I made a down payment. And I know you plan to hold me accountable for the balance due! So, give me the keys to *my property!*"

When this type of exchange, however, is translated to the modern workplace, it is met by an older generation, many of whom did not attend college but worked their way up to such prestigious positions as those expected to be obtained by what they consider to be "unseasoned youth," or those who haven't "put in their time." As so often is the case between these age groups, friction results. Elders cite such negative attributes as "entitlement," "a demanding attitude," or even accuse individuals of being "green;" while younger folks feel underappreciated and unjustly limited, desiring to be "given more leadership/authority."

STUDENT LOAN PAYMENTS: MORE DIFFICULT THAN PROJECTED

While the scenario I have outlined, as it pertains to real estate, seems absurd, it is sadly a very realistic one where the graduating student is concerned. Considered in conjunction with the fact that student loan payments can be astronomical—nearly impossible to make on regular, entry-level wages—a person can feel threatened by a workplace that doesn't immediately offer the financial rewards a student was counting on. Often, the delay between graduation and obtaining high-end, prestigious, or coveted positions is not realistically represented when the decision about whether to pursue secondary education is being considered. Students expect to go straight from receiving a degree into the job they want. Beyond this, students often underestimate the future competition they will have for these desired jobs, and at times they're overwhelmed by the high number of other people seeking the same position.

Upon graduation, students are further thrown for a loop by their student loan payments that are now due that cannot be included in bankruptcy or otherwise discharged. So, regardless of how financially desperate they become, they're permanently burdened with the debt until they are able to pay it off. Furthermore, those who have taken a break from school (longer than six months) are saddled with this debt despite their lack of degree, meaning that entry-level wage earners must make student loan payments equivalent to the payments required from actual graduates, who use higher, post-educational salaries to make such installments. For these, re-enrolling in school is much easier said than done for multiple reasons, resulting in a larger population that likely will remain living in their parents' homes until a solution surfaces, and whose likelihood of defaulting on student debt repayment will now increase. For many, the total owed for master- or doctorate-level degrees can be near $500,000, with monthly payments soaring upwards of several thousand dollars a month, and with high interest rates that keep the balance climbing unreasonably.[191]

One borrower, Colette Simon, now sixty-five years old, who financed a doctorate degree for $200,000 in the early 2000s, has now paid $90,000 toward her student loan, but despite these payments— thanks to late penalty fees, high interest rates, and other factors—the balance due hovers over $400,000 and she now fears that her Social Security income will be garnished.[192] Simone said, "If you want to get ahead, you have to go into debt. And then the whole debt structure is rigged to make sure you're never going to get out of it." Unfortunately, that has been the experience for many who have attended college, regardless of whether they have graduated.

Furthermore, starting wages haven't risen fast enough to offset average debt at graduation,[193] meaning that the debt-to-income ratio continues to increase, even for those who complete their continued education. Of this sad dilemma, Toby Merrill, director of the Harvard Law School's Project on Predatory Student Lending, said, "Predatory colleges target the same low-income populations that the subprime mortgage boom targeted by offering a similar promise of white picket fences and higher education as a part of the American middle class dream."[194] Beyond this, "a recent analysis by the Urban Institute found that a 1 percent increase in student debt decreases the likelihood of owning a house by 15 percentage points."[195] Likewise, entrepreneurship declines because debt ties individuals to the need for a safe, reliable salary, which drives those who may have taken risks that coincide with starting a business to opt for traditional employment.

A THRIFTY GENERATION

Allow me to present a new label for Millennials, and for a change, *this* one is not offensive or derogatory: "thrifty."[196] A Motley Fool's article published by *USA Today* in November 2017, stated that while this age group does not save as much in actual dollars as their older counterparts, they *do* set aside a larger percentage of their incomes than previous generations. This story elaborates on results of a recent Merrill Edge Survey report, stating: "8% of respondents saw Millennials as 'very good savers'—compared to 54% for seniors, 45% for Baby Boomers, and 19% for Gen Xers. Yet that same survey revealed that Millennials are actually saving *more* money than older generations, in terms of the percentage of their annual incomes they set aside."[197] It appears that many of those living with parents are making good use of the opportunity to practice frugality. The story continues: "Given their lower salaries, rising living costs, and high levels of student debt…it's impressive that Millennials actually save a higher percentage of their paychecks than older generations. The notion that they spend too much on food and entertainment, require instant gratification, and live off their parents might be based more on stereotypes than reality."[198]

Ironically, the insertion of technology into society, while responsible for presenting some obstacles to our youth, may actually be contributing to this trend. It has offered the availability of budgeting tools and apps, which many claim to use.[199] Furthermore, the "quick-click availability" of price comparison and product reviews via online search engines makes it easier to make educated purchases. In fact, a recent study showed that 71 percent of Millennials practice comparative shopping before buying, and more than half do so while they are still in the store.[200]

Beyond these factors, the DIY ("do it yourself") movement is increasingly popular with today's young adults. Many surprisingly beautiful pieces of furniture—built out of discarded wooden pallets!—are surfacing in homes everywhere. The shabby-chic motif seems to be here to stay, and interest in antiques is ever-mounting. "Junking"—a term recently coined to describe scouring flea markets, estate sales, antique stores, and garage sales in search of items that are still usable, has become the prerequisite for another new popular activity: "repurposing." This, in turn, is the new craze of consisting of recreating something new out of an old, discarded item whose parts are still salvageable.

When it comes to the economy, Millennials have been dealt a bad hand, the culmination of many elements set into motion *long before they were of age*. In all fairness, it they seem to have made the best of their situation. Their ability to save money, their willingness to live at home with parents into their own adulthood, their frugality in shopping, and their participation in such activities as "repurposing" prove that they have embraced the current state of economic affairs with optimism, ingenuity, and adaptability. In light of such an endearing response to an unfair set of circumstances bestowed upon the Millennial generation, I'm compelled to ask:

Why aren't such positive attributes as *these* touted when we speak of our modern young adults?

Similar Needs, Different Backgrounds

Millennials are, in many ways, no different that the preceding generations. Surely, all humans have the same basic needs and desires at the core of their being. Furthermore, many of the practices held by our youth, when viewed with the proper perspective, show that even their material needs are similar to those of older groups. However, a dramatic shift in the economic, sociocultural, and political climate—not to mention the methods of communication and the sheer speed at which they do so—has contributed to a setting wherein the demeanor of the young is easily misread. Ever present in the background of all of theories about our up-and-coming generation is a universal truth that is often overlooked, yet is valid: *Young people are zealous.* Whatever they decide to be, they do it with all their might. The adventurous search for dangerous extremes; the professionals seek to climb the corporate ladder all the way to the top; the artists pursue even the deepest corners of their mind in search of creative revelation. Even if a young person is *lazy*, he or she will likely be *ultimately* so.

Millennial Kelly Williams Brown spoke at Ted Talks of Salem in January of 2014 as an advocate for her generation. During her address, she made a valuable point using audience participation. She started by instructing all members of the audience who were over twenty-one to raise their hands into the air, keeping them in place. She then said, "If between now and the time you were 21, you have become somewhat less self-centered, less self-focused, keep your hand in the air."[201] A few hands may have descended, but the camera view of the audience revealed that the large majority remained stationary. The next prompt the young speaker gave was to tell the crowd members to keep their hands up if their values have changed since they were twenty-one. This was followed by a similar direction, this time posing the query of whether each person had accomplished and achieved everything they once imagined that they would.

The young woman then said: "Okay, congratulations: Your 21-year-old selves are all Millennials, or, as some people like to say, '*young people*'."[202] The statement was met with a good-natured laugh from the audience, but there is validity to her words.

The onset of youth's zeal is initially encountered without the balance of experience. And to some degree or another, every generation contends with this. As a young adult ages, understanding changes and adapts, expectations adjust, and wisdom increases. The countereffect of this is often that people become tired, settled into routines, and all-too-willing to forget how passionate they once were. Kelly Williams Brown's statement sums up the quandary that ensues when youthful zeal and mature adjustment reach the point of friction: "This is the thing about all of these critiques [those made by older crowds regarding youngsters]...we [those observing the youth] always have to sort of collectively wring our hands over young people being young, and wonder why they can't just have the benefit of maturity and hindsight."[203]

Yet, when surveyed, many within our youngest generations have values that older people find noble. When young adults were asked their most important life aspiration, the most popular answer—at 51 percent—was to be a good parent, while 30 percent responded that it was to be a good spouse.[204] This is more than 80 percent of those surveyed stating that family is a top priority. The third most popular answer was to be a vital member of their community.[205]

There's that word again: "community." The desire for community is perhaps the most commonly articulated desire posed by Millennials. Yet our population lives under continual division that is often imposed by our societal setting. During these times the church should rise to the occasion and envelope these individuals, giving them a place to expend their enthusiasm and engage their passions while offering mentorship and guidance as they embrace inclusion and vitality in an organization that does fulfilling, long-lasting, and ministerial work. However, stated previously in this book multiple times, the religious institution is rapidly losing this younger audience. We need to investigate the reasons for this exodus, yet, it's difficult to put a finger on exactly what those leaving churches are unhappy about. As stated at the beginning of this book, efforts like making over our facilities or introducing new programs don't seem to be at the heart of the solution. The remainder of this book will be dedicated to identifying and resolving the issues that are driving a large part of an entire generation away from church.

6

THE COMMUNICATION GAP
BETWEEN MILLENNIALS
AND THE CHURCH

AT THE END of the previous chapter, we briefly discussed the Millennials' departure from the church and made short mention of their need for community. The point has been made repeatedly throughout this book that often, when a young person asks for something or states a complaint, there is often a deeper issue than the mere surface-level comment or question relayed. Thus, when we ask why our young people are leaving religious institutions in great numbers, answers don't always touch on the real problem. Even when churches adapt their facilities or services to try to retain the youth and young adults, it is not uncommon that still have an ever-dwindling congregation. Yet, the departure remains mystifying. After all, the young collective repeatedly requests community involvement—and what better place for that than the church?

What if we could get beyond this confusion, peel back the layers of miscommunication, and get to the heart of the matter so that our young people can obtain precisely what they're asking for: involvement in a motivated, earth-changing, needy-reaching, relationship-building *community*? Surely this would launch an outpouring of the Holy Spirit unlike any this world has ever seen. It is true that this generation is a powerful, passionate, and massive entity that could turn the world upside down for good if their efforts were coordinated in a movement of the gospel. However, one somber reality remains, which serves as a gargantuan obstacle to this exciting scenario (and for which is the purpose of this book): Millennials are leaving the church *en masse*. While this young and capable generation of activists searches for a cause, the church finds itself closer each day to hosting an empty auditorium, the minister addressing an audience that has all but vanished. We are so close, yet so far away, from a sweeping movement of the Holy Spirit—all at the same time.

Hanging in the balance is a generation of valuable souls and a church that holds the key. Unfortunately, however, it is as though the key is located on a ring with a hundred others and the proprietor often doesn't know *which* one accesses *which* door. While our youth evacuate from the churches, those observing scramble to halt the exit and retain members (and save souls). Many in leadership fumble frantically, testing one key after another, but are unable to come up with the right one to change the events unfolding before their very eyes.

IT'S NOT YOUR FACILITY, IT'S YOUR EFFORT

The issue of how to update your church facility or programs in order to make Millennials more welcome is the topic of many books—likely as a response to the same issue that inspired this book. For this reason, the amount of space dedicated to the subject of the *actual facility* in this book will be limited; however, a few things do bear mentioning before we delve into the underlying issues. As young adults repeatedly assure churches that the *facility* is not what lies at the heart of their desire to attend or not, many maintain that the effort made by church staff sends a different type of signal than the actual building. With this in mind, there are a few practical ways to relay to young adults that their attendance matters to your organization, and that repeat visits on their part are worth an investment of your time.

PREPARING YOUR FACILITY AS UNTO THE LORD

For many individuals who regularly attend church, it can seem difficult to understand how the facility can limit its growth. Certainly, when a group is fired up, ministering to their community, and pouring all their efforts into reaching the lost, the congregation is bound to grow despite material limitations. However, when it comes to the issue of making your church's facility the very best that it can be, Thom Rainier makes a statement regarding a church's attitude about presentation that is worth repeating:

> They see the issue from a gospel perspective.... They want facil-
> ity that is safe and clean. But they have a bigger vision than that.
> They realize many of the guests will not be followers of Christ.
> And if the leaders of the church can demonstrate they care about
> the safety of those who visit, those guests may very well return.
> And they could very well hear and respond to the gospel.[206]

Your church may verbalize the words "we care," but the quality with which you prepare your building is what provides proof. Again, the emphasis is not on a structure's size, location, age, or flashiness, but rather on its ability to convey that the people who make up your church body are invested in doing the best they can with what they have.

Have a Website

Like it or not, we're living in the age of technology. For this reason, if it is possible for your church to build a website, it is a worthwhile investment. A recent survey showed that 55 percent of Millennials see the Internet as a useful tool, stating that information they find via this means influences decisions that they make.[207] Many individuals in search of information about programs, service times, or other details regarding your organization will try to find answers online. Considerably fewer folks will take the time to place a voice call to get the information. In fact, in Thom S. Rainier's book, *Becoming a Welcoming Church*, he reports that "seven out of ten guests will go to a church website as a determinative factor in where they will choose to visit."[208] If details about your church—from its doctrinal statement and profiles of church staff members to starting times and parking directions—cannot be found online, you're potentially limiting your audience.

Check Your Nurseries and Restrooms

Due to increasing awareness in recent years regarding the spread of germs, Millennials are particularly aware of cleanliness. A strong argument does not need to be made here: A simple look around the room in nearly any setting yields bottles of hand sanitizer, bleach wipes, and other such disinfectant measures not present a decade or two ago. State and county health department regulations continue to become more stringent on facilities of all types, and the perpetual introduction of new or modified bacteria and viruses remains a central source of concern for individuals throughout society.

If your facilities are not updated with the most expensive building materials, don't fret. The key issue is to ensure that the facilities you *do have* are clean and orderly. Subliminal messages speak quickly and powerfully to our young people (another byproduct of their advertising exposure). For this reason, clutter, mildew stains (even on a disinfected surface), poorly stocked restrooms[209] or other signs of neglect will speak volumes. Even subtle touches such as lighting make a big difference; a dimly lit church may feel outdated and dusty[210] in contrast to the crisp, bright illumination offered in modern buildings.

Furthermore, this especially important in your nursery and other areas designated for children. Rainier notes:

> This response generated the most emotional comments [among first-time visitors]. If your church does not have clear safety and security procedures, and the children's area does not appear clean and sanitary to the guests, do not expect young families to return to your church. Indeed, as word about your children's area grows, do not expect young families to visit the first time.[211]

This issue is particularly essential where security is concerned. I know of several families with children who decided whether to return to a church based on their confidence that their child was safe and in good hands in the nursery, and that they *personally* would be the only individuals allowed to remove their child from that setting. Beyond this, it goes without saying that all children's department workers should be of good repute and fully screened, including criminal background checks.

THE MODERN, "COOL" CHURCH

It has been stated previously that in an attempt to retain their young audience, many churches have made efforts to make over their institutions, adding coffee shops, replacing classic hymns with contemporary worship music, updating buildings and facilities, and adding nontraditional programs to their repertoire. While these measures show a gallant willingness to invest in youngsters, they somehow come up short as it pertains to the momentum of our young crowd, leaving many staff members assessing which metaphorical key to try next. Ironically, many young adults acknowledge the attempts made by modern churches, but claim that their reasons for leaving stem from completely different issues than the things that many religious institutions are currently overhauling in response to their departure.

Could it be possible that, while many Millennials cite *one* issue as being their cause for walking away from church, there is a deeper, underlying issue for each reason given? As we've already established, there is a bit of a language barrier in the generation gap. After all, many older people feel as though, when Millennials spell out their reasons for leaving the church, conflicting culprits are pinpointed. How then, can the church respond, when they sometimes seem to contradict each other? We will discuss this in the upcoming pages of this book.

Below are some frustrations that youth today say they have with the church. They are put off when:

- Leadership is insincere.
- Young people's participation is not welcome, allowed, or valued.
- There is a lack of concern for the poor and/ or needy.
- The church condemns the culture.
- The members are cliquish and unwelcoming.
- The church is resistant to change.
- There is a lack of compelling vision.
- There is a lack of financial transparency.
- The church will not tackle critical or controversial issues.
- The church is old fashioned or patriarchal
- The church is not unified.
- There is an emphasis on entertainment rather than on discipleship.

For many, this may seem like an exasperating list of contradictory issues. For others, the immediate response is that the church has already unsuccessfully attempted to address these matters. For example, the church tries to "tackle controversial issues" might be accused of "condemning culture." Equally, those showing their readiness to embrace change may likewise be accused of "emphasizing entertainment over discipleship." While each grievance seems to polarize on one end of the spectrum or the other, there has to be a middle ground wherein the true seeker finds the elusive answers that lie behind the veil.

Because many of the complaints that young adults have about the church are interconnected, this list will not be addressed item by item as it appears above, rather, each will be touched upon as context allows throughout the entire chapter. We have organized our own list of what we believe are the underlying issues and will thus address each individually.

RESISTANT TO CHANGE

Many churches that have overhauled their buildings, programs, and even leadership in an effort to reach a leave-taking youth will object to this label, yet it remains a complaint cited by many young adults. Online author Frank Powell's viral Internet article, "10 Reasons Churches Are Not Reaching Millennials," states that a key factor is the effectiveness of the change in question: "Millennials don't hold traditions close to their heart. In fact, for many…traditions are often the enemy because many churches allowed traditions to hinder them from moving forward.… Millennials are tired of hearing the phrase 'this is how we have always done it.'"[212]

Because the youth of today are so motivated to see results when they put forth any kind of effort, it often agitates them to see tired or outdated events continue when an update might be more effective. To them, it is a waste of resources and a lost opportunity. A previous generation may have held dear the methods rendered by time-honored customs, but Millennials move quickly, and every dollar, moment, or other resource spent without yield is one that they are hasty to overhaul.

But, what type of change are they looking for? As already stated, many churches have updated their buildings and programs, but with little result. In fact, a knee-jerk reaction seems to be off-putting to the younger generations, because they come off as not being authentic. In contrast to this, 67 percent of Millennials stated that they prefer "classic" church to "trendy," and 77 percent, when given the option, choose a "sanctuary" over an "auditorium."[213]

So when and where does this "change" need to take place, and when does it make an institution appear "unauthentic"? This is a subject churches must discuss case by case, but some insight is available. Another grievance voiced by young adults is that their involvement and/ or feedback is either ignored or unwelcome. Many have even suggested that church leadership should take the time to engage in intentional conversation with their young members, inviting their feedback, in an attempt to find what is lacking. As each congregation has different strengths, weaknesses, and demographics, each likewise has varying talking points. Prayerfully deciding within core church leadership what can be changed about the institution, while committing to keep scriptural truth intact, can give churches a place to start.

That brings us to an important point: When deciding to restructure church practices, certain activities and practices must remain. When we discuss doing away with outdated traditions, it is vital not to confuse them with essential sacraments that are a part of our faith. Of these practices, Millennial author Rachel Evans states:

> What finally brought me back [to church], after years of running away, wasn't lattes or skinny jeans; it was the sacraments. Baptism, confession, communion, preaching the Word, anointing the sick—you know, those strange rituals and traditions Christians have been practicing for the past 2000 years. The sacraments are what make the church relevant, no matter the culture or era. They don't need to be repackaged or rebranded; they just

need to be practiced, offered and explained in the context of a loving, authentic and inclusive community.[214]

LACK OF COMPELLING VISION

This complaint seems to go hand in hand with the issue of willingness to change tradition. As stated previously, the resources (especially time) of young adults are precious commodities, and when they feel that such resources are being spent fruitlessly, they'll quickly make a change. Millennials want to believe they're part of an enormous movement, and they want to *dream* it with those who share in such efforts. A church that will engage in planning and future-building makes the youth of today feel like their investment contributes to a larger, grander-scale picture. Nearly any young person will tell you that he or she wants to change the world. What better place to do that than through the church? It may seem to go without saying that a church needs a vision. Likely, every church has some sort of mission statement in its bylaws, but many attendees are never made aware of the written infrastructure of the institution. In this way, there is some significant communication gap between the government of an institution and its congregation. While the answer to this may not necessarily be to hold church business meetings in a public forum during the Sunday-morning service, it may behoove any congregation to be made aware that such documents exist and are available upon request.

Furthermore, one may quickly find the written bylaw is not—in and of itself—the answer to this conflict, either. After all, having mission statements and bylaws in a dusty folder in the church office is certainly no guarantee that the institution still practices it—let alone dreams it. Many Millennials complain that too many churches are content with the unexceptional. This generation wants more than to join a group of onlookers who warm the pews once a week. They want to take the nation by storm and be followed swiftly by the rest of the world. They are motivated and want to see exciting changes take place. On this issue, Frank Powell comments: "Good or bad, [Millennials] have a strong desire for the extraordinary.... Failing and being a failure are mutually exclusive. They dream often and dream big because they understand they serve a God who works beyond their abilities. Millennials have a collective concern for making the world a better place, and mediocrity fits nowhere in those plans."[215] These people want to see a fired-up collective willing to leave their comfort zones behind and start making some waves.

LACK OF VULNERABILITY/TRANSPARENCY AMONG LEADERSHIP

According to the Barna Group, "the median age of pastors is 54, yet the largest living generation in the United States are [M]illennials."[216] In response to the retreat of young adults from churches in recent years, many of these institutions have overhauled pastors' and other leaders' dress codes, permitting more youthful attire: earrings on men, skinny jeans, etc. Unfortunately, for many, this transformation often comes through as unauthentic. After all, the opportunity to engage with members of church leadership who are older is an opportunity for mentorship, in which case, people don't need to try to seem younger than they are, but rather to "own" the age they are while accepting, loving, and investing in members of other age groups.

This is often where the complaint about entertainment taking a priority over discipleship comes in. Many have disdained modern churches for coming across as "fake." They want religious leadership built of individuals who are trustworthy, who have integrity, and whose personal lifestyles throughout the rest of the week match the message they send when they are at church. It has been stated previously that this is a particularly intelligent generation of young adults who (because of large amounts of media, particularly advertisements) have learned to make quick judgments based on very little data. With this in mind, it is easy to understand that fraudulent personalities are a quick turn-off, especially given the Millennials' aversion to institutions in general and their passion to change the world for the better. A leader who is not authentic is wasting status and resources that, in the mind of a young adult, should be spent reaching the community and helping the needy.

Likewise, large, flashy but unauthentic worship services; grandiose but insincere sermons; or leadership personnel who do not "practice what they preach" are repellent to our young adult churchgoers. Furthermore, the days of church leaders keeping up the façade of having a "perfect life" is over; the young people want to follow ministers who face human struggles and trials just as they do. Jesse Wisnewski elaborates: "Millennials aren't interested in you being perfect. What they're interested in is whether or not you are willing to share the struggles and temptations you face, and how your faith in Christ influences how you handle these situations."[217]

LACK OF MILLENNIAL INVOLVEMENT

Much like the situation with Millennials in the employment setting, young adults are frustrated with the fact that they're not more involved in church leadership. This presents an issue for many churches that defer to placing more seasoned members in these positions. The conundrum is as follows:

A young adult decides to become involved in church. After attending for some period of time, he/she volunteers to serve in a leadership capacity. Recalling that time moves much more quickly for members of the younger generation than for the older, it's likely that the time the young adult has spent attending seems adequate, but, the older member may feel that the young person hasn't "put the time in," so involvement is minimized or overruled. The Millennial is off-put by this rejection and attendance declines (or stops completely), while the older person's response may include accusations such as entitlement.

There are two sides to this coin. On one hand, the younger generation is made up of those who *really* want to be involved in a community—one that does lasting, important work. What better place to engage in this than at church? As stated previously, identity, generativity, purpose, and legacy drive the innermost part of our beings, and these are the passions that make our lives feel meaningful. Naturally, those who ask to be involved in the work fostered by a church will take rejection of such a request personally and respond negatively. Furthermore, as has already been stated, these young adults have seen thousands of ads in their lives, giving them the ability to form opinions quickly and decisively. These are extremely intelligent, analytical thinkers. Because of this, they see through any attempts on the part of church leadership to divert their efforts toward tasks they deem less important or less visible. What I mean is this: If a Millennial asks to serve in an elevated position in church leadership and instead is placed in a smaller, less noticeable post, church leadership should give one reason only: the truth. If we attempt to patronize young adults by giving a "softer" reason for the reassignment, they will see through it. However, explaining, with love, the church's position regarding accountability, experience, prerequisites, or other decision factors may render surprising willingness to work up to the previously requested position.

On this matter, Frank Powell comments: "If you want to push the next generation away from your church, don't release them to lead.... They want to be trusted to fulfill the task given to them. If you micromanage them, treat them like a child, refuse to believe they are capable of being leaders because of their age and lack of experience, wisdom, etc., they will be at your church for a short season."[218] He explains that the determined young adults of today will not allow their age to keep them from doing an effective job at anything they set their mind to.

On the other hand, church government is a sensitive issue. Leaders must be trained, proven in both knowledge and integrity, and "seasoned," as unfair as some may believe this to be. Others may surprise you, as mentioned previously, by being very understanding once they are openly and honestly communicated with. Seasoned ministerial front-runners are all too aware that matters can spring up unexpectedly within a church that require quick, discerning, loving, and scripturally-founded action. While God is fully capable of bestowing all of these attributes on a moment's notice to someone who has been called on some critical, situational uprising, it is only prudent to screen and train those who ask to be involved in the institution's proceedings. For this reason, there are no perfect solutions to this dilemma.

The best way to handle this issue is found in an honest approach and by having bylaws and policies set into place that are well thought out and have been prayed about. Most churches have such an infrastructure; these are often updated and voted on by members or staff, but it is surprising how many attendees are not fully aware of them. This can—believe it or not—be a large part of the problem. The action to take, then, is to be certain to communicate these rules to the congregation, particularly to those who show interest in becoming involved.

If you're a minister who is pulled into multiple directions, it can be hard to find time for such conversations with individuals, but this can provide a solution for this issue. When young people show interest in being involved in leadership, visit with them in a small group, *really hearing* what that mission is. Ask questions about why they see themselves performing a particular role, and take time to explain the types of training and experience it requires. If it is necessary to start with a simpler job before taking on the requested role, explain why, while stressing that the smaller jobs are preparation for the larger one: "He that is faithful in that which is least is faithful also in much: and he that is unjust in the least is also unjust in much" (Luke 16:10).

Examples of this are found throughout the church: the Sunday school director was possibly once the person who cut out craft supplies; the food ministry director was surely the dishwasher, the facility director may have at one time been the custodian, etc. Millennials want to be involved where their skills, talents, and attributes will be part of a bigger picture. In fact, "77% of Millennials said they are more likely to volunteer when they can use their specific skills or expertise to benefit the cause."[219] For this reason, many individuals (and this is not limited to the Millennial generation) aspire toward visible jobs. This is not necessarily because they want the prestige, but rather because it is a job they *noticed* being done and were able to connect with their own skills and experience.

Condemnation of Culture/ Not Tackling Tough Issues

On one hand, religious institutions are criticized for condemning the culture. On the other, churches are judged for neglecting to tackle tough issues. A third angle reveals that some churches look down on nearly all aspects of society, finding fault in secular music, fashion trends, television shows, activities and even hobbies, while others refuse to make a statement on any of these issues, citing salvation as the only topic worth discussing—and is it any wonder, considering the complicated factors that influence all characteristics of modern society? Many churches grow silent on what they consider secondary issues, opting instead to focus on retaining every soul who commits to church attendance. There is a profound element of wisdom in this approach. Yet, Millennials are passionate and motivated; they want to know that when they open up to Scripture, they're being given the whole story. Their "inner radical" isn't interested in attending church to warm the pews; they want to know engage with a group of people who operates according to a set of life-altering convictions.

There isn't an easy strategy here, nor is there one answer that each young person will find palatable. As discussed earlier, an individual's right to choose and nurture his or her own truth has become a mainstream privilege seized by many members of society, and for others, privatization has become an increasingly popular approach. But what happens if and when the church resorts to privatization? The results will either be an empty sanctuary where the gospel is preached exclusively to the "already saved" or a largely attended club where biblical principles have been abandoned. Likely, both will be devoid of a young audience. The heart of the issue must be understood by churchgoers, and thereby will likely be a factor helping them decide whether to continue to attend. That central point is this: Those who follow God's law are called from the beginning to be set apart from the rest of the world: "But ye are a chosen generation, a royal priesthood, an holy nation, a peculiar people; that ye should shew forth the praises of him who hath called you out of darkness into his marvelous light" (1 Peter 2:9).

Furthermore, Jesus Himself explained during His time here on earth that we are not of this world when we are His followers: "They are not of the world, even as I am not of the world" (John 17:16).

Since the beginning of mankind's time on earth, there has been some social division between those who follow God's law and those who don't. Some issues simply are what they are, and sadly, there is no pleasing everyone.

Additionally, many churches adopt a legalistic view toward the culture around them as a protective shield against what they perceive to be an invisible invasion of evil that could somehow permeate their congregation. Certainly, church leadership has a right and responsibility to attempt to shield their flock from influences that may contradict God's outlines for Christian life. However, even in His time on earth, in His dealings with the Pharisees Jesus condemned the legality of the law when it is presented without God's love (Luke 37). Many don't like the concept of being held to a legal, biblical standard, yet many claim the reason they left the church has to do with teachings conflicting with scriptural truth.

While Millennials, at times, cite frustration when they don't believe the church is teaching what the Bible *truly* says, they are likewise exasperated when religious institutions condemn the culture. The bottom line is that if the Bible endorsed every activity going on today, America's churches would be full—standing-room only—across our nation. The brutal truth is that there are things going on within our society that the Bible does not authorize. Simultaneously, those who shy away from what Millennials call "tough issues," opting for more "generic" subject matter, are quickly spotted and branded for their timidity. Millennials are smart enough to identify such a sidestep and bold enough to call out an institution for employing such a tactic. How can the church juggle such a multifaceted conundrum without offending people, losing members, and compromising scriptural truth? Is it even possible? A few guiding principles might help narrow the gap on this one.

1) **Know your Bible.** When someone asks you about something having to do with your faith, know how to find the answer and show that person where Scripture addresses the matter. If you don't have the answer, be honest (remember, these young adults can spot a tall tale a mile away) and tell them you'll look into it. One primary complaint is that church leadership doesn't seem transparent enough. Imagine how far it would go with a young adult to say there is something you need to learn! It would likely disarm much hostility for a young person to realize as a church leader, you also have your own vulnerabilities. Taking the time to research the matter and follow up will demonstrate that you listened and that you care about the person.

2) **Love people and let God be the One to show them what needs to change.** We've all heard the phrase: "You can lead a horse to water, but you can't make him drink."[220] In our own power, we can never make others change; that's between them and God. Similarly, it's all too easy to point out the flaws in the lives of others: "Or how wilt thou say to thy

brother, Let me pull out the mote out of thine eye; and, behold, a beam is in thine own eye?" (Matthew 7:4).

It is the church's job to deliver the gospel to those around us, to relay biblical truth, and to be a supportive fellow-Christians. Loving individuals and forgoing judgment of them allows the Holy Spirit room to convict and guide according to His will. On the other hand, defensive individuals are often less open to hearing God's voice. Judgment only fortifies the argument/position of others and thus contributes to the problem rather than solving it.

3) **Employ prayer.** If you have to tackle a tough issue, begin by asking for prayer from trusted confidantes and church advisory personnel. If a person asks a question that might become confrontational, tell him or her that you will pray about it and follow up. If addressing the question in a public format such as a Bible study or sermon is not appropriate, a small group setting might be best. Dodging the question completely is likely to have adverse effects. Present the statements you feel led to make in love, back them scripturally, and pray that the Holy Spirit will work on individuals privately. Talk *through* the issue, showing compassion, and acknowledge those who are hurting as a result of the matter. Many people find that they can handle the truth when they feel that they have been heard and the message is spoken in love.

In 2016, Recklessly Alive ministry's Sam Eaton wrote an article entitled "12 Reasons Millennials Are Over Church," wherein—through somewhat confrontational language—he attempts to explain to church leadership the decline in attendance of youth. Despite the hostile responses Eaton received, there were valuable nuggets of truth in his article. On the matter of churches talking about difficult issues, he stated: "People in their 20s and 30s are making the biggest decisions of their entire lives: career, education, relationships, marriage, sex, finances, children, purpose, chemicals, body image. We need someone consistently speaking truth into every single one of those areas…because these topics are the teaching millennials are starving for."[221]

Beyond this, our young generation is not afraid to mingle with culture, and it frustrates them when the church is. Again, Frank Powell offers insight: "When the faithful saturate their schedules with Christian events at Christian venues with Christian people, the world has a hard time believing we [Christians] hold the rest of the world in high esteem."[222] Because our youth are jaded with mistrust of most institutions, they want to see the church break out of the molds that previously confined it to venture out into the streets and mingle with the lost—not just stand within a sanctuary waiting for the stray to wander in. As Powell put it: "Millennials are not looking for perfect people.... Jesus already handled that. Millennials are looking for people to be real and honest about struggles and temptations."[223] Powell likewise challenges the church to mingle with culture, showing love to all, thus following Jesus' example: "Millennials are increasingly optimistic about the surrounding culture because this is the model of Jesus. He loves all types of people, does ministry in the city, and engages the culture.... The goal of Christian living isn't to escape the evils of the culture and finish life unharmed. To reach people today, the church must be immersed in the community for the glory of God."[224]

LACK OF COMMUNITY

As old and tired as this statement may seem to some, it is still an often-repeated issue amongst many churches: Some places don't feel welcoming. Whether it is an attitude of judgment, an unwelcoming spirit, or a size that is either too small and cliquish to fit in or too big to feel intimate, there are always reasons for many to feel out of place in church. Many churches have follow-up cards on which visitors are invited to leave contact information for future communication, while others have welcome hosts inside the front doors who give out bulletins featuring details about Bible studies, worship services, small group gatherings, and other opportunities for involvement. These are all good ideas, but when people don't feel at home in church, a deeper problem is at work.

Someone who is looking for community is looking for a place to *belong.* This is a complex need that cannot be satisfied with a quick handshake or a copy of the church bulletin. Often, when visitors enter a religious facility, they're looking for one of two things: spiritual life intervention during a critical moment or peers and mentors with whom faith is shared and who can help them navigate life situations or engage in activism. Recall that today's youth are the most isolated and lonely generation on record. Yet, it is a biblical foundation stone that we need each other, and that this necessity for faith-based relationships becomes stronger as time progresses: "And let us consider one another to provoke unto love and to good works: Not forsaking the assembling of ourselves together, as the manner of some is; but exhorting one another: and so much the more, as ye see the day approaching, (Hebrews 10:24–25).

The size of a group doesn't matter; it's the quality of the bond between people that decides whether a Millennial—or anyone, for that matter—will stay in a church. In a Barna Group survey, when members of this generation were asked to "describe their 'ideal' church by choosing between two opposing terms, ... 'community' and 'privacy,' the vast majority of millennials (78%) chose community."[225]

Furthermore, once people become a part of your congregation, they continue to need to feel as though they are a vital mechanism in a larger machine. If they ask to help, find a place for them to serve. If they ask about a particular Scripture or life issue, follow up with them, letting them know that they have been heard. I believe that feeling needed is one of the main things young adults are looking for. If our religious institutions don't fill that need, there are secular ones that will. We can't afford to drop the ball on this one. Furthermore, if they weren't seeking this type of interaction, they would likely opt to watch services via online streaming from the comfort of their home. The fact that they are showing up *in person* is a testament to their need to be involved with your church body.

Rachel Evans, online blogger and author of *Searching for Sunday: Loving, Leaving, and Finding the Church*, in her article entitled, "Want Millennials Back in the Pews? Stop Trying to Make Church 'cool,'" referred to involvement in the church as being part of an "ancient-future community."[226] This phrase sums up what so many young people are looking for: Something that is older than they are and that will outlive them. It is bigger than entertainment, more important than fashions and trends, and farther-reaching than politics. It's not just seat-warming, it's church attendance with a *purpose*. A religious community that can latch on to *that* concept will gather many young adults to be part of its movement.

Consider Powell's contribution to the conversation regarding the importance of this interaction:

> The next generation desires a Christ-centered community. Community keeps Millennials grounded and focused.... Challenges them to reach heights never imagined alone. Jesus lived in community with twelve men for most of His earthly ministry... spent a lot of His time pouring into people [note how the concepts of community and mentorship intertwine]. Community isn't an optional part of a Millennial's life...it is essential.[227]

Powell explains that this type of involvement made a vital difference in his own life, helping him to find his life path and gain victory over sin and trials, and motivating him to have a fuller life in God—even through ministry. Again, the link between mentorship and community is evident.

Another, subtler hindrance to attracting and retaining a congregation that can be rectified by a stronger sense of community within the church body is a byproduct of many young adults these days postponing marriage and starting a family. When many people imagine church-going people, they envision a father, a mother, and some children. Author Jana Riess commented on this in a recent article, "Why Millennials Are Really Leaving Religion (It's Not Just Politics, Folks)":

> One of the biggest demographic trends of our time is that millennials are delaying marriage or not getting married at all. And since there's a strong correlation between being married and being involved in religion, the fact that fewer Americans are getting married is worrisome news to clergy.[228]

Similar statistics show a connection between parenthood and religious involvement: The fewer children people have, the less likely they are to be involved in a church. This likewise compounds the delay caused by postponed marriage. Churches readily offer programs for families to attend together, or that extend childcare/parent-divided events. In contrast, it is not always guaranteed that individuals belonging to such demographics as singles beyond high-school age, professional women, couples without children, etc., have a place to "belong." Often, this is because of declining numbers of attendees within the same demographic, and results in placing people in classrooms or events geared toward members of a different (usually older) age group. If a church is strongly motivated toward mentorship, intermingling subsets can become an engaging and fulfilling (rather than awkward) experience for the younger folks.

CHURCH NOT HELPING THE POOR

In the 2016 article referenced earlier, "12 Reasons Millennials Are Over Church," writer Sam Eaton, stating that the church is not doing enough to help the poor, offered this solution: "Survey your members asking them what injustice or cause God has placed on their hearts. Then connect people who share similar passions. Create space for them to meet and brainstorm and then sit back and watch what God brings to life."[229] The backlash against Eaton for the article was even more strongly worded than his original article (which pulled *no* punches), but he made some valid points. Unfortunately, as is often the case in communication between the younger and older generations, the strong, icy words in much of the article were met with defensive verbal counterattacks, and the vital issue was lost in translation.

Furthermore, there is a dual position regarding this issue. One evolves from a "bloom where you're planted" stance. Many feel that God has placed their ministry right in front of them, so they apply their efforts toward their daily interactions and routines. Examples of this are parents who invest in their children; high-school teachers who try to live upstanding, inspirational lives; waiters and waitresses who privately pray for customers and throw in "God bless you!" whenever they get the opportunity. For them, ministry opportunities are all around and they believe the global approach to missions begins at home: "He answereth and saith unto them, He that hath two coats, let him impart to him that hath none; and he that hath meat, let him do likewise" (Luke 3:11).

When Jesus said we should meet the physical needs of others, the passionate Millennial takes this order literally. Hence, when they see people filing in and out of church on Sundays, yet they don't witness any of these individuals engaging in activities such as volunteering at food banks, funding or attending mission trips, or participating in other types of outreach, many think the churchgoers have forgotten or neglected this teaching.

Yet another variable must be brought to our attention, and that is a point made by G. Shane Morris, who wrote an equally passionate article in response to Eaton's. Morris stated:

Two-thirds of people who frequently attend religious services make regular charitable donations, and 60 percent give to religious and nonreligious charities other than churches, especially basic social services for the needy, combined purpose charities (like United Way), and healthcare. By contrast, fewer than half of those who don't attend regular religious services support any charity.[230]

He fortifies his argument with such points as the fact that those who typically volunteer for religious causes donate more money than those who volunteer for secular and that "half of all American personal philanthropy and volunteering is distinctly religious in character."[231] He even states that low-income contributors who claim religious affiliation match in percentage with offerings made by the wealthy. So what is likely the crux of this three-way dilemma? "But when thou doest alms, let not thy left hand know what thy right hand doeth" (Matthew 6:3).

In Eaton's article, he shares his disdain for money donated to churches that is never accounted for. "Why should thousands of our hard-earned dollars go towards a mortgage on a multi-million dollar building that isn't being utilized to serve the community or to pay for another celebratory bouncy castle when the same cash–money could provide food, clean water and shelter for someone in need?" he asks.[232] This single statement drives home many points that this book is attempting to make: 1) The communication between age groups is, at times, hostile; 2) Millennials are a passionate generation of activists who want to serve the forgotten and can change the world if pointed in the right direction; 3) Millennials aren't afraid to confront what they think is wrong; and 4) There is a communication gap between church leaders and many regular attendees.

On a similar note, because of our youths' aversion to institutions, private ownership is often something they're often guarded about as well. Right or wrong, most young people these days favor communal benefits to private gains. While the ramifications of this preference—on an economic basis—is potentially disastrous, their thinking coincides well with the handling of church finances. The distinction as to whether a communal financial effort is healthy manifests in whether the consideration is a private individual operating for personal success or a benevolent organization operating under the heading of doing something to help the needy (typically, nonprofit organizations). Many young people recall some point when misappropriation of ministerial funds or other fraudulent activity caused private, personal gain for one or few individuals or when funds or resources in question *should* have gone toward the good of many. For this reason, any time communal monies are solicited for the claimed cause of making the world a better place, young people are likely to inquire boldly about the usage of those resources.

All things considered, it is possible that the individual who makes claims that both churchgoers and the institutions themselves do nothing or very little to help the poor are unaware of efforts being made. After all, those who give from a religious standpoint likely also do not advertise it, according to biblical instruction. For those who want to find out about giving that is done by the church, some information should be made available upon request. Those who are concerned that contributions are not being made appropriately should investigate before making accusations.

Another vital point in this conversation is the fact that many who operate within their private world "as unto the Lord" are indeed following God's calling for their lives, and to assume they're not passionate about the needy could be a false charge. Not everyone who cares for the poor does it in a visible way. I used to work at a school, and I knew a particular teacher who, upon learning of a child in need, would privately meet that need anonymously. An onlooker may have believed that she did nothing to care for the needy, but this would have been only due to the teacher's subtlety. She purchased such items as school supplies, winter coats, shoes, a basketball, and even once paid off a student's lunch charge account, but few people were ever aware of this activity. Not everyone's contribution is entirely visible.

That there should be no schism in the body; but that the members should have the same care one for another. And whether one member suffer, all the members suffer with it; or one member be honoured, all the members rejoice with it. Now ye are the body of Christ, and members in particular. (1 Corinthians 12:25–27)

Some people fulfill God's calling for their lives each day through their regular responsibilities, whether in their profession, their family, their neighborhood, or elsewhere. Others are called to more visible occupations. When dealing with those who voice frustration over a (perceived) lack of care for the needy and poor, patiently describe some of your church's outreach missions and find a place where they can get involved. (If your church currently isn't doing any mission-oriented functions, then maybe your inquisitor can kick-start that ministry for you!) The passion and conviction shown by the young person who demands that God's orders be followed can be indicative of a fearless and revolutionary spiritual leader. Handling such matters with love, honesty, and mentorship can make the difference between whether a person leaves the church in exasperation or leads it in the next revival.

LACK OF MENTORSHIP

Good news: Our youth of today want to be mentored! As Eaton's article notes, "Millennials crave relationship, to have someone walking beside them through the muck."[233] He points out that Millennials hold the highest percentage of fatherless homes ever, and that what today's youth really needs are "mentors who are authentically invested in our lives and our future."[234] Beyond this, he reminds readers that today's young adults are missing the sense of being personally valued, the knowledge that they're good enough, and the feeling that their contributions are indispensable and helpful. Despite the fact that communication about this type of involvement can become lost in translation between the younger and older age groups, one who is watching for this request often begin to see it consistently surfacing, as it is a recurring theme in society's unspoken language.

Millennials are looking for adults who are willing to engage with them. Because such a large percentage of this generation was raised in fatherless homes (rendering a single mom dividing her time between childrearing and working full time), many of these are surprisingly open to the wisdom of older people. Unfortunately, this communication is often sabotaged before it is even able to be nurtured because of the defensive lingual style between modern young and old generations. Consider Powell's insight: "While [Millennials] do not like paternalistic leadership, they place a high value on learning from past generations.... They value wisdom and insight. It is a valuable treasure, and they travel long distances to acquire it.... If your church is generationally divided and refuses to pour into the next generation, you can be sure your church will not attract Millennials."[235]

Unfortunately, many people are intimidated by the idea of mentoring a younger person, falsely believing that they are somehow unqualified. We will discuss this at greater length in the next chapter, but for now, consider this: Even if you are asked a biblical question that you are uncertain of how to answer, this is a great opportunity for you to learn learning alongside a younger person. As stated previously, be honest about what you don't know and make it a matter of investigating God's Word together. This is one way the age gap can finally begin to work *for* a group instead of against: each generation has their own means of researching. The technological age offers myriad tools for biblical interpretation, and the older people who have the patience to work with a young adult can begin to appreciate more greatly the advantage of multiple points of view and different ages. Because of the individuality of each contributor, all angles of discovery will foster a varying perspective, creating a more well-rounded study.

With this said, a young person (or group of them) will likely enjoy exploring these things together, each approaching biblical truth, but employing his or her own angles, thus engaging in a collaboration. Perhaps one person will point out the financial aspect of a scriptural interpretation while another may recognize a unique political dynamic and yet another person notes a cultural element influencing the meaning. Being a mentor involves an equal investment of friendship and teaching, and honesty may open the door to a whole new level of relationship between older and younger individuals. Beyond this, author Nancy Flory reminds members of the older generations that young people need to feel like their contributions are vital and the "church should be open to 'reverse mentoring'... This means asking Millennials to share knowledge about how to 'navigate life in this digital age,' and reciprocal sharing between generations."[236]

A recent study by the Barna Group showed that "young people who have an older mentor from their faith community are 59 percent more likely to stay in church than those who do not."[237] People who fall inside this age range are asking significant questions that pertain to purpose, legacy, and the meaning of life. When mentorship provides a place for the individual to actively participate in the greater operation of community, it serves a person's sense of identity and legacy. Furthermore, when mentorship and community are tied into a religious foundation, answers to questions related to the meaning of life are satisfied as well. Scripture assures us that mentorship and community involvement are essential in the body of Christ, activated and effective:

> But if we walk in the light, as he is in the light, we have fellowship one with another, and the blood of Jesus Christ his Son cleanseth us from all sin. (1 John 1:7)

Now we exhort you, brethren, warn them that are unruly, comfort the feebleminded, support the weak, be patient toward all men." (1 Thessalonians 5:14)

WHAT MILLENNIALS REALLY WANT: TO SEE THE BODY OF CHRIST AT WORK

When all of the factors covered in this chapter are considered, it all comes back to one issue: Young people want more than to attend an institution that meets at a specific time and place once a week. They want to be involved in a *movement* and to be part of a cause larger than themselves, one that reaches farther than they ever could on their own. Are they really that different from the rest of us? Certainly, their communication style can be. Because of the speed at which they often make their point, strong opinions lead and supporting nuances can be lost in the mix, resulting in quick, decisive statements that some people find offensive, thus making them miss the *core message being relayed*. I hope that throughout this chapter, some of these conflicts have been smoothed out and their truer meanings exposed.

Millennials have made it known from the beginning that what they want in a church is primarily includes the following: They want to have leadership that is honest and that has integrity; they want to be involved in ministry and even in leadership within their own church; they want the gospel to be the heart of every mission; they want caring for the poor to be a high priority; they want unconditional love to be given to all who attend; and they want the church to act as a unified community and to treat each individual who comes to visit or stay as though he or she is a vital part of that mission.

This is excellent news! Millennials want exactly what Jesus wanted:

Neither pray I for these alone, but for them also which shall believe on me through their word; That they all may be one; as thou, Father, art in me, and I in thee, that they also may be one in us: that the world may believe that thou hast sent me. And the glory which thou gavest me I have given them; that they may be one, even as we are one: I in them, and thou in me, that they may be made perfect in one; and that the world may know that thou hast sent me, and hast loved them, as thou hast loved me. (John 17:20–23)

Now that we're all on the same page, let's get started…

WHAT MILLENNIALS REALLY, REALLY WANT

WHEN WE SORT THROUGH the mixture of signals being sent and messages being relayed between generations and get to the crux of the Millennials' disdain for religious institutions, we find that the answer is really much simpler than it seems. Beyond this, the exciting news is that what they ache to see happen is precisely what churches are likewise praying for.

Millennials are asking for one thing: To see the church activate in a new, sweeping momentum that changes the world and effectively reaches the lost. In a word: They want *revival!* They want to see tired, old traditions clear the way for fresh, modernized—but still biblically sound—worship of God. They desire to see the body of Christ emerge from dusty, archaic buildings filled with empty pews and begin to work on the street with those who need God most. These individuals are motivated not only to *witness*, but to *partake* in the modern-day re-enacting of stories such as the Good Samaritan, wherein a stranger saves the life of a man with no ulterior motive (Luke 10:25–37) and the tale of the loaves and fishes, wherein Jesus feeds the multitudes while simultaneously ministering to their souls (John 6:1–14). Beyond this, Millennials are a bold collective who will call what they perceive as a lukewarm church out on the ultimatum given through the account of the sheep and the goats (Matthew 25:31–46).

In their own way, members of the younger generation are taking a stand against religious complacency, challenging the church to stand up and fulfill the duties given to those who call themselves the Lord's sheep. They are generationally minded and community-oriented activists who—for better or for worse—have drawn a line in the sand, making the following statement to the church: Take righteous action in a hurting world or we will go somewhere else where this principle is practiced.

As stated many times throughout this book, many churchgoers heartily agree, and even state they're already doing all they know to do. However, is there more that can be done? The answer is likely yes. In this way, a message from our youth can be an enlightening communication to the older generations, and the reverse is likewise true. For the young, the world can be viewed as a place to seize both risk and triumph, with hopeful anticipation placed on the years ahead. For seasoned adults, a few trial-and-error lessons have likely made them more hesitant to jump right in to challenging new scenarios. They carefully apply resources, cautiously weigh their options, and more accurately estimate any consequences. This wisdom that comes from additional years of experience, but it is sometimes misinterpreted by the young as apathy. There is strength in the positions of both the young and old, and when combined in the presence of God, the two have earth-changing force. When these two worlds collide, each generation will see the sweeping presence of God's hand as it glides across our land.

At the center of the message, what our youth of today really want is no different than any other generation has wanted. In truth, while their environmental, economic, political, cultural, and societal setting is *completely unique in the history of the world*, their basic human needs are *no different than those of any previous generation*. These individuals want to be part of a community where their contributions are worthwhile and lasting, where they feel like they have a place to truly belong, where enduring, quality relationships are forged, and where their sense of purpose thrives. Ladies and gentlemen, these have been the heart's desire of nearly every man and woman for the entire history of the world. The only differences in this generation pertains to their circumstance and communication style.

> And it shall come to pass in the last days, saith God, I will pour out of my Spirit upon all flesh: and your sons and your daughters shall prophesy, and your young men shall see visions, and your old men shall dream dreams. (Acts 2:17)

God promised to pour His spirit out on our sons and daughters. Don't you think this passionate, young generation is primed for this? Note that this Scripture says that the young will prophesy and the old will dream dreams; this means that each age group has a place in the kingdom of God as it works, prophesies, and envisions together. However, this God-ordained destiny will manifest differently amongst our youth than it will in our older population. When our mature collective sees a zealous and youthful crowd, we should not be off-put *or* intimidated—we must perceive the visionary ambition in our youthful population as an asset that can we can mentor and channel into the kind of momentum that changes the world—fulfilling the *very thing* that young people, themselves, are asking for and exactly what we older churchgoers have been praying for. This is mutually beneficial between age brackets, and is specifically how the kingdom of God is meant to operate.

A MILLENNIAL BEFORE HIS TIME

Keith Green was a secular musician who signed his first record deal at age eleven, but he was initially unsuccessful due to his young age. His teen years were spent in a tumultuous search for truth that "led him to drugs, eastern mysticism, and free love."[238] After meeting and marrying a woman named Melody, Keith found Jesus, and his life changed radically. He and Melody immediately opened their home to the lost: addicted folks who needed a place to get off drugs, homeless people who needed shelter, or people who were simply in need. All were welcome to stay at what became dubbed as "The Greenhouse."[239] Last Days Ministries (LDM) reports that, beyond offering shelter to strangers, Keith showed such generosity as to begin the "'whatever you can afford,' pricing system for some of his music (even if it meant giving it away)… And, long before TOMS [shoes], he embraced the 'buy-one, give-one' model, requesting that Christian bookstores that sold his album give another to the customer for he or she to give to a friend."[240]

Keith's music changed over the course of this time to reflect his own, passionate pursuit of God. LDM notes: "Keith was thrust into a 'John the Baptist' type ministry—calling believers to wake up, repent, and live a life that looked like what they said they believed."[241] He even stated that, had it not been for hypocritical Christians, he may have personally found God sooner than he did.[242] Keith himself told believer: "If you praise and worship Jesus with your mouth, and your life does not praise and worship him, there is something wrong!"[243]

That sounds like some of the statements made to our modern churches by the Millennial crowd, doesn't it? In fact, many declarations made by this revolutionary Christian artist, along with his life's actions (such as giving things away and opening his home to outsiders), follow closely the type of passion displayed by our current, modern youth. The more radical Keith became, the more the once-struggling artist grew in popularity, until he eventually performed free concerts to crowded stadiums hosting as many as twelve thousand people.[244] And, as his passionate, pull-no-punches messages were delivered to the throngs, "thousands upon thousands"[245] were led to the Lord during the closing altar calls. During one of his final tours, Keith's expressed the urgency for Christians all across America to leave their comfort zones and venture "into the world to reach the hurting."[246] His ministry centered around the types of people who would likely never darken the doors of a church: those addicted to drugs, members of red-light districts, men and women in prison, and other needy folks found on the streets.

In 1982, a plane crash took Keith Green to be with his Lord. Yet, more than thirty-five years later, the imprint he left on the world through his Christian music and ministry remains. His fervent pursuit of the kingdom of heaven still resonates with individuals who hear his music and story today. The bold statements rendered through his music, though similar to the statement of a current Millennial, are remembered with a fondness now extended to the modern youth making a similar declaration. Of his own faith, Keith wrote with brutal honesty and vulnerability, as is shown through the following excerpt from his song "My Eyes Are Dry":

My eyes are dry, my faith is old.
My heart is hard, my prayers are cold.
And I know how I ought to be,
Alive to You, and dead to me.[247]

Keith's frustration was not limited to himself, however, and he was vocal about it. His exasperation with complacent believers was glaringly obvious through the church-challenging lyrics of another song he wrote, entitled "Asleep in the Light":

Do you see, do you see, all the people sinking down.
Don't you care, don't you care, Are you gonna let them drown.

How can you be so numb, not to care if they come?
You close your eyes and pretend the job's done.
"Oh bless me, Lord, bless me, Lord," You know it's all I ever hear.
No one aches, no one hurts, no one even sheds one tear.
But He cries, He weeps, He bleeds, and He cares for your needs,
And you just lay back and keep soaking it in.
Oh, can't you see it's such sin.[248]

As stated previously, this man died more than three and a half decades ago. He was twenty-eight years old at the time—a young adult. The fervent exasperation at lukewarm faith relayed through his lyrics was very similar to that voiced by many Millennials today. Likewise, it is a recorded fact that many of Keith's audience members squirmed[249] as he challenged them to leave their comfort zones. While our current young population is largely more vocal than previous ones, individuals like Keith Green make a case for the prospect that youthful zeal exists in every generation and is often precisely how God operates in extreme effectiveness when His followers surrender to His will and place enthusiastic action behind their words and intentions.

Interestingly, statements made about the Millennial departure from the church seem to echo the era from which Keith Green emerged. See what Nancy Flory of The Stream had to say regarding this issue:

> It would seem that all of the effort put into large, elaborate, flashy and overdone churches have been all for naught. Millennials are the hippies of the Christian movement; they want simple and honest Christianity in a utilitarian and natural space where they can rest and connect with a very real and authentic God; they crave relationships and connections with older adults, drawing from their wisdom and insight; and they want a participatory experience where they have a seat at the table in shaping the church of the future—their church.[250]

What Millennials want—and the request that is between the lines of all their grievances about the church—is for the church to provide a place where their faith can become grounded and intertwined with relationships and earth-changing action. This collective desires to join a Bible-believing community where the parameters of faith are clearly outlined, giving them something solid to stand on. Then, they want to form lasting and constructive interactions with those around them, giving their own established faith the opportunity to manifest in real-life applications, not merely in abstract ideals listed on a piece of paper. Finally, they want to act upon these principles and values by taking that momentum out into the world, fulfilling the Great Commission.

AGE GAP HINDERING CHURCH UNITY

Much of the tension between age groups is often derived from opposing perspectives on similar issues. For example, members of the older generation become frustrated with those in the younger generation who live at home with their parents, while the former take a defensive stance, sometimes even stating that the economy "tanked" under the previous generation's watch, and they struggle as a result. Another illustration: Many Boomers are annoyed with the lack of opportunity to invest in youth around them, feeling as through their advice is unheeded, while the younger group, when offered counsel, feels as though they are being judged and thus recoils. This communication gap seeps into our churches—for instance, when a young person is told there is much that needs to be done for the kingdom, but then is not entrusted with responsibility after volunteering. These conflicts cause the youth to search for other ways to expend their energies. Sadly, the secular world is chock-a-block *full* of just such opportunities.

The Importance of Mentorship

At this point, it should be more than clear that the position of this book is that Millennials are looking for involvement in a community. But author Aaron Earls sheds further light on the urgency of this issue:

> This generation, more so than any other, recognizes the cultural costs of being a Christian. It's no longer the cool thing to do. Because of this, they want to walk with others as they follow Christ. Millennials want to pour out their lives into others and find strength in numbers. Churches that provide an avenue for this will connect with this generation.[251]

This sounds like a desperate plea for righteous, deep, and lasting friendships and relationships. Beyond this, it serves as the single most vital argument for mentorship within the church. With the younger generation's understanding that interaction with Christians is "no longer the cool thing to do"[252] and yet their desire to be included in that same community, it seems only natural that those who are more mature—those who can offer advice, comfort, and guidance *along with* friendship—should take them by the hand and steer them through these tumultuous waters. Statements made by Millennials themselves acknowledge their need and desire for mentorship. In fact, even in the workplace, where a great deal of age-related friction currently exists, 79 percent of young adults *still* reported the preference of a professional mentor.[253]

The Power of Vintage

One only has to look around these days to see the renaissance of interest in all things vintage. Trends (influenced by economic stressors and fascination with the technology of days gone by) embrace thrift wherein old meets new. We are seeing furniture built from shipping pallets, restored muscle cars of the 1950s and 1960s, and roller-skating to dubstep (a modern, computer-generated psychedelic rock) music. Even the sweeping steampunk movement features new creations made from pieces of older articles (things such as cogs, springs, and gears that would have been discarded as trash two decades ago). Those who previously might have donated an entire collection of LP records to the Salvation Army may now find that they can sell them for upwards of $20 each, depending on the artist and condition of the item. Additionally, participation in hobbies and trades that previously showed decreasing interest, such as knitting, tatting, and blacksmithing—is now again on the rise.

It has been previously mentioned in this book that a young person does not necessarily need to see an older person trying to be hip or act younger than their age. Without even realizing it (however unqualified one may feel), the more mature adult innately has something the younger one wants. These aforementioned trends show the desire to connect with generations that have gone before. The reason for this is likely something young people would have difficulty articulating, yet their desire to bond with the timeless exists because it connects them to heritage. Recall that this is the most fatherless generation in history. Millennials are missing something very dear to their hearts and are seeking assembly with that elusive element. Through your investment, you can show members of our young population precisely what God meant when He said He would be "A father of the fatherless" (Psalm 68:5). The means by which you offer to connect may be extravagant (depending upon your resources), but more likely is a smaller gesture. The key is to be *available*.

Stop thinking that the problem is too big—or worse, that the youth of today are unreachable. They've made hundreds of public requests for mentorship: a simple Google search of this subject is proof. We owe it to them not to give up on them. The deed that launches interaction can be as simple as an act of kindness. Talk with young people. Remember their birthdays. Ask them how school is going. See if they have New Year's Eve plans. Walk your dog with them. Sit with them at the laundromat while they wait for the dryer cycle to finish. Ask them to introduce you to their favorite genre of music. Then, bring out your old LPs and player—young people love this type of thing. There are many skills and hobbies that older generations take for granted that young people have never even had the opportunity to enjoy, such as sewing, building model cars, making cookies, or operating power tools. It can literally be as simple as *doing what you already do, but with company.*

Likewise, don't assume that you'll get an instant response. As awkward as it may be to try to foster a new friendship that reaches across generations, it likely will be awkward for them as well, although it has the potential to be equally and *eternally* rewarding. Start small: pay for their sandwich at Subway and allow them to leave or sit elsewhere without feeling obligated to visit with you while they eat. Never underestimate the life-changing power of even the smallest gestures. Avoid—at *all costs*—fostering an us-versus-them attitude about different age groups. Young adults have heard enough older people slamming their generation; be the *one* person who is encouraging for a change. Find nice things to say or attributes to compliment.

Before passing judgment, remember that God promised to pour out His Spirit out on our sons and daughters, as stated earlier in this chapter (Joel 2:28, Acts 2:17). This shows that our young people are extremely important to God and thus to His Body. Furthermore, it illustrates that He has plans for their lives, which makes it our responsibility to reach out to them in a way that they can respond to. Cling to biblical beliefs, but don't use them as weapons. After all, Jesus used the Word to breathe life into people, but the Pharisees used the Word to intimidate and tear people down. When young people say things you don't relate to (or that possibly even sound absurd), assume that you've misunderstood and inquire further. Likewise, gently share your perspective as opportunity arises. Remember, you have the power of being "vintage." Your point of view may be one they've never heard, and if they're not defensive, it is likely they will be open to it or at least will hear you out.

After a very short time, what an older person may have initially taken for a young person with an attitude problem could very well begin to sound like an individual who has simply experienced a different world. With mutual goals in mind—those aimed at making the world a better place—there is common ground that can be shared between generations, regardless of life experience. And, while you are waiting for the opportunity to share the gospel, continue to study God's Word and pray that He will impart His wisdom to you at the appropriate moments: "Study to shew thyself approved unto God, a workman that needeth not to be ashamed, rightly dividing the word of truth" (2 Timothy 2:15).

Many have seen church functions or outreach events using the phrase "Won by One." This has become the slogan for many mission trips, Bible studies, and devotionals, and it's even the name of a Christian southern gospel band that was active in the mid 1990s and early 2000s. The expression itself, albeit a bit overused, still holds a timeless truth. It is true that one has the power to move many, and those looking for a way to make a difference in the world act in little ways every day. We can create a domino effect without even realizing what we are launching when we look for small ways of sowing seeds of love and positivity in our daily interactions.

The simple "pay it forward" movement taking place these days is one example of an organic up-springing of actions that show the widespread desire of individuals to connect with others. Generally, it looks like the following scenarios: Driving through a fast food restaurant, a random stranger pays for the order placed by the car behind him; a person or family in a diner is told by the server than an anonymous benefactor has paid their bill; when in line to pay for items at a convenience store, a nearby stranger tells the cashier to add another individuals' items to her total. In fact, this very thing happened on the trip home from Virginia that I spoke of at the beginning of this book. Donna Howell and I were treated to bottles of water purchased by a stranger. (Ironically, we had been discussing this very point in the car only minutes before.)

Simple acts of kindness such as these are daily proof that we have a population of individuals seeking relationships with each other, regardless of their ability to put that desire into words. When we act similarly, we open opportunities for conversation that the Lord may lead into life-changing appointments.

THE MESSAGE CROSSES GENERATIONAL BOUNDARIES

When I was a teenager, I helped in our local church's children's ministry. On any given Sunday, this group included anywhere between forty-five to sixty-five children ages five through twelve. I'll never forget the first time I looked on as a sweet, gentle man named Dave Hoard stood up in front of the throng to read to them from a Christian adventure story. There were few pictures in the book, so pages of mere words comprised the bulk of the content.

Dave was the kind of man who spoke gently to all children, even when they had done something wrong. During discipline, he did not condemn, but encouraged them to transcend former mistakes, acknowledging that *he knew* that they could do better. He called the boys names like "champion," and referred to the girls with endearments such as "lovely." He spoke life into each youngster he encountered. On this particular day, I was certain this meek man was about to be eaten alive by the mob of rowdy kids present. As this humble and kind man lifted the book and cleared his throat while positioning himself in front of the microphone stand, I noticed several of the boys in the back row begin to giggle mischievously. My fear for the man mounted, as did my assumption that a novel could surely never keep the attention of these ruffians. After all, these students were used to watching television, running around outside, or playing Nintendo (the craze at that time). I never dreamed they would sit and listen as Dave read from those pages. And for the first few moments, they didn't.

Then, a transformation took place, one I've never seen from an individual reading a book to children before or since those Sundays with Dave Hoard. This man engaged so wholeheartedly in his reading that he brought every character to life. He was so enthusiastically invested in the storyline that as he regaled those children before him with his words, they were quickly drawn into his tale. It may seem hard to believe, but this crowd was awestruck, hanging on his every word. Then, after some time, he did the unthinkable. He paused dramatically, and said, "And we'll leave it right there until next week."

The groan that collectively emitted from his audience taught me something that day: Even after time has moved on from a certain *method of delivery* (in this case, a novel), when a message is delivered with sincerity, enthusiasm, and love, no generation or technology gap can stop that force. The message of love transcends the obstacle of means.

THE UNSPOKEN MESSAGE RELAYED OVER TIME

Likewise, I'll never forget a couple named Eugene and Evelyn Fuller (we kids called them Grandpa and Grandma, even though there was no blood relationship). They mentored our entire family when I was little, and there's not enough space for me to begin to cover the extent of their involvement. For the purposes here, however, I can discuss briefly the time I spent with Grandpa. During the summer, he would take me and my brother for walks through the small town of Amity, Oregon. We would stride slowly down the sidewalk while he told us silly stories until we reached the end of town, which was at the time, roughly ten to twelve blocks away from his house. Then, we would walk back. Sometimes we did this more than once a day. Afterward, he'd take us in his house and play one round of tic-tac-toe after another. I don't know how long these sessions would last, as a child's perspective of time doesn't always coincide with real-life minutes and hours, but I recall spending enough time on this activity for the sun to descend significantly during our session.

Evelyn, Grandma, was equally involved in our lives, often teaching me how to sew or cook. We always enjoyed being with this elderly, outspoken Christian couple; they had a way of making us feel like we were important—special, even. Ironically, the message of their esteem for us was never conveyed through lofty, overly complimentary words, but rather was relayed through the investment of their time. Now, as an adult, I have an entirely new level of appreciation for Grandpa's willingness to share these hours with us and for his patient attitude while enduring countless rounds of the one-dimensional (I dare say mundane) activity that is repetitive, endless tic-tac-toe. Throughout the remaining years of the Fullers' lives, every member of our family knew that if we needed help, resources, godly advice, or just a friend, either of one of them was there for us. This is the kind of connection our modern youth is looking for, and sadly, many have lived without.

THE ULTIMATE MENTOR

Jesus' perfect example is one to bear in mind. When He walked upon the earth, He mingled with people of all walks of life without allowing their lifestyle to permeate His. He was consistent in love, forthright with truth, and gentle in delivery. Young people of today are asking to be mentored by—and involved in a community with—individuals who conduct themselves in this way.

A Face-Off with God's Love

In the beginning of this book, we discussed two works entitled *The Cross and the Switchblade* by David Wilkerson (the movie and the book). A person who is familiar with either of these may believe they understand the whole story. After all, these works embody Wilkerson's own retelling of the scenario. Yet, it is not until we hear from the notorious gangster Nicky Cruz himself (the young delinquent with whom David Wilkerson worked so hard to foster a relationship, thus leading him to the Lord), that we can really understand the other side of the story, which consists of what transpired in Nicky's heart over the course of these interactions.

David Wilkerson faced Nicky courageously, presenting no timid version of God's unwavering truth and His love for mankind. This extremely angered the young delinquent, who wanted nothing to do with God's love. Wilkerson's message was one of truth, hope, salvation, and love, but Nicky's background—one of high exposure to witchcraft and violence, as will be elaborated on within the following pages—had left him with the impression that all spiritual beings were malevolent and wanted only to hurt people. Thus, he thought Wilkerson was making a cruel attempt to spread an evil lie.

Cruz later described this young preacher as a "skinny, white guy"[254] who had the audacity to preach right in the middle of the notorious gang member's turf. Cruz was so enraged by Wilkerson's presence—and more so, by his *message*—that he spat on him, cursed him, and threatened to kill him.[255]

Wilkerson's brave response was, "You could do that, you could cut me in a thousand pieces and lay them out in the street and every piece would love you."[256]

This daring, life-changing exchange between David Wilkerson and Nicky Cruz lasted only a moment, but it held crucial significance for each of their lives' stories and subsequent ministries. While this young, vulnerable preacher—completely out of place in such a setting—stood unwavering, willing to die for the message he carried, something in each man's core shifted.

Of this moment, Wilkerson later said, "It was really something I was proving to myself. I didn't want to stay within the four walls of the comfortable church.… I didn't want to talk about the Holy Ghost unless I could see it change the lives of the worst. And here was my opportunity. Most of the guys did not mock, but Nicky, *he* was mocking. I think that was the cover up for the hurt that was inside. My grandad said [that if] you throw a stone at a bunch of dogs…the one that gets hit yaps. And Nicky got hit by the Holy Ghost, and was yapping."[257]

Nicky Cruz, on the other hand, *hated* hearing about God. The very words caused his anger to boil, and his immediate response was, as stated previously, to threaten to kill the young preacher. The communication recalled Nicky's mind to his upbringing in Puerto Rico, under his parents' involvement in witchcraft. His father was a Curandero, a healer in his homeland whose powers were derived from dark supernatural activities. Nicky's childhood exposure to rituals, evil spirits, and severe domestic abuse had caused him to believe that all spiritual beings existed to torture and oppress people. This belief, combined with bitterness and anger harbored from an intensely abusive childhood, caused a violent aversion to the preacher man's message to stir within the young gangster.

When Nicky heard David Wilkerson talking about God, he was immediately suspicious. The young delinquent did not know what "god" the preacher was speaking of, or what kind of dark and sinister power the man might be selling. He *did* know, however, that he wanted no part of it, and he wanted this individual off his turf, *immediately*. In his indignation, Cruz explains that the god of *his* father was violent. This entity was responsible for countless incidents of abuse, of anger, of *hate*.

But when the young preacher stood there, face to face with the criminal, willing to give his own life for the sake of his message being delivered, something in Nicky Cruz budged. The former delinquent tells, in his own words, how God transformed his life through that single moment when David Wilkerson responded to his death threat with love:

> He said, "Look, you can go ahead and kill me, and cut me into a thousand pieces. And you can throw them right there, on the street. But remember that every little piece will cry out, that Jesus loves you, and I love you." And that hit me hard. That was when I saw the boldness; something different.... That's when I froze. He [Wilkerson] did something to me. He took my guard away, he disarmed me. Because I was now dealing with the greatest force of all forces: the love of God. Because I do believe with all my heart that there are two kinds of love: the human love and the divine love. And when these two elements get together, something supernatural happens in the human being's life. And the only way that I [could] really feel that there is a God was [through] the touch of a human being. It wasn't a storm or bricks.... Wilkerson was the element; the human element.... I saw the love of God through this man; that he wasn't afraid to die for something that he believed.[258]

In the beginning of this book, I discussed my conversation with other Skywatch personnel in Virginia on the night when Tom Horn asked me, "How do we get to the place where the Millennials says, 'Keep it up, Preach. You're coming through?'"[259] Little did he know that a deeper search into the same situation would yield the answer to this very question.

The answer, as Nicky Cruz himself put it, is the *human element*. It happens at that moment when an individual sees the love of God at work through another human being. It transpires when a person is willing to leave behind his or her comfort zone, step out on a limb, and invest in someone else, regardless of the cost.

That is how we finally get the message of God's love to come through.

David Wilkerson went on to become a Christian evangelist, and as mentioned earlier he launched and directed the ministry Teen Challenge (a Bible-based addiction recovery program), and served as founding pastor for the Times Square Church in New York City. Nicky Cruz likewise became a Christian evangelist, started a ministry entitled Outreach (out of which developed the mission TRUCE [To Reach Urban Communities Everywhere]), and even served as the director of Wilkerson's Teen Challenge for a period.

Because of this singular moment when unwavering truth in the message of God's love was delivered from one man to another, thousands upon thousands of lives were changed over subsequent decades through *both* individuals. So, is this to suggest that we reach Millennials by living in our cars on the streets of New York and trying to talk to gangs, as Wilkerson did just before he met Nicky Cruz? Not by any means. There was no ideal "formula" that the young preacher followed in order to land where he did other than to surrender his life to the will of God and make a decision to invest in others. Each of us has a unique way that we can become that "human element," as Nicky Cruz refers to it, to someone near us.

Anybody who has even briefly studied the Scriptures can see that God has made a statement of love for His people. But, as in the case of Nicky Cruz, some people need a physical, tangible representation of God to help them replace their preexisting concept of a distant, faraway being who has no daily practical application in one's life, or even worse, who is possibly considered a threat. For some, it is not until a human being reaches out to them and puts action into place, combined with God's message of love, that they are able to fully grasp it.

God's love doesn't come on our terms, it comes on His. This is how people of all generations can easily get off track. It does not arrive through our own efforts, regardless of how gallant or self-sacrificing we are. On the contrary, the moment when a life is transformed can be a seemingly simple: a mere instant implemented because of an individual who has surrendered to the will of God and follows His instructions, no matter how risky (or fruitless) the orders may seem. The conversions of lives are often the product of an act of unwavering faith by individuals who place themselves solely under the direction of God. The given instruction may not always make sense, and it's likely to be inconvenient. (While Wilkerson was beginning his street ministry, he followed God's orders one day at a time. In the beginning, he even slept in his car, while his pregnant wife was at home in Pennsylvania, nearing the time of childbirth. This man knew what it meant to follow God's direction despite uncertainty. However, he allowed the love of God to lead his footsteps.)

THIS LOVE CHANGES PEOPLE

This type of love comes through the spiritual power of God—it is entirely unlike human love—which is precisely why it is life-changing, with results lasting longer and reaching farther than any other kind of love. It far surpasses romantic love, brotherly love, even parental love. God's is a love so compelling that when people experience it, they begin to change because it is undeniable and powerful. This is how the Holy Spirit compels people to righteousness. When we act under the power of the love of God, others feel an influence so strong that human arguments become petty and diminish. Making a case for one's own stance no longer matters, because one who has experienced God *wants* to be in line with His will. Long-lasting changes that take place often are initiated privately between individuals and God. They act in response to the supernatural love that has been bestowed upon them. While some people need to see and experience this force acted out through other human beings, once it has taken hold, people are forever changed by its power. The transformation begins:

Therefore being justified by faith, we have peace with God through our Lord Jesus Christ: By whom also we have access by faith into this grace wherein we stand, and rejoice in hope of the glory of God. And not only so, but we glory in tribulations also: knowing that tribulation worketh patience; And patience, experience; and experience, hope: And hope maketh not ashamed; because the love of God is shed abroad in our hearts by the Holy Ghost which is given unto us. For when we were yet without strength, in due time Christ died for the ungodly.... But God commendeth his love toward us, in that, while we were yet sinners, Christ died for us. (Romans 5:1–6, 8)

LEARNING THE LANGUAGE

One obstacle we face, both as individuals and as a church, is learning to speak the language of the Millennials. This, of course, is much easier said than done, since their communication style is often relayed instantly and is both blunt *and* riddled with nuance: the consequence of their seeing thousands of ads per day. The best starting point is to lay aside defensiveness. Each time communication seems off-putting or hot-tempered, it helps to recall that many of these young people are literal communicators. Often what in previous eras would be broken down into several smaller talking points and relayed carefully so as not to offend is merely blurted out—in real-time—by the today's young people. I'll give you an example.

I had promised my twenty-two-year-old son that I would go paintball with him. He was attending a huge paintball event in a town located a few hours from where I live. He had previously texted me a message saying: *We have to start at 9 AM.* I sent a return message saying: *I'll be there!*

The next morning, I arrived at 8:45 ready to go—or so I thought.

When I got out of my car, I was approached by my son, who frantically made his way toward me. "Where have you been? We start in fifteen minutes!" I was mystified, because I had thought I was early. After some conversation, he blurted, "No, Mom, I didn't say *get here* at nine…I said *we have to start* at nine. You still have orientation, gun check, hydration check, injury-release forms to sign, and the ride out to the field ahead of you. We'll never make it in time now—the whole battle will be over before your pre-reqs are done!" His agitated demeanor made sense now; he had meant we were to *start the actual battle at nine*. However, there were multiple prerequisites required in order to be allowed on the battlefield that I had been unaware of. Because of this, the *actual* start time had been lost in translation.

With this new understanding, I began to ask questions about the schedule for the next morning's paintball battle to ensure that we did not repeat this scenario. Our communication became very businesslike—very literal and we emphasized details.

"What time does the *actual battle start?*" I asked, articulating sharply for the sake of clarity.

"Nine AM" came his no-nonsense reply. Each of us fostered assertive body language—not because we were angry, but because we were each, in turn, relaying details that were of crucial importance.

"OK. What all *must happen before* we can leave for the battlefield?" Again, my words were crisp. He answered, giving details in a similar manner of speech. Simultaneously, our eye contact remained intense as we gave our full focus to the conversation.

A nearby, older man who witnessed this exchange thought we might be having some sort of confrontation, and he interjected, asking if we were all right. We laughed, said that all was well, and explained *why* we often resort to communicating in such a manner. However, to this bystander, our language and tone had seemed sharp. Between us, it was not a matter of hostility; we were just making sure *details* were clearly expressed. Had we begun this conversation using similar tactics over the phone, and not collaborating through text, there likely would have been no miscommunication in the first place.

The following day, I arrived in plenty of time to complete all requirements before the battle. My son and I had a blast paintballing together and riding in a helicopter over the battlefield. We made an epic memory and made plans to do it again someday.

However, this is a perfect example of how communication can go awry between age groups. On one hand, a younger person who is a literal communicator sent a short message through a digital interface—a technology and communication style a person of my age is still catching up to and, as a result, sometimes misinterprets the message (as in this case). Nearby, an older man looking on presumed that a confrontation was taking place and decided to try to help. We were a triangle of miscommunication: a young person (my son) whose message wasn't heard correctly, a middle-aged person (me) who did precisely what she thought she had been asked to do and still had missed the mark, and an older person (the nearby man) who believed he was seeing some kind of conflict and decided to take matters into his own hands. My son and I laugh about this story often, but it is a very good example of how communication between age groups can cause unintended friction that can escalate quickly.

Members of the older generations need to learn the language of the young. This requires setting aside defenses and investigating the motivation and meaning behind communication—verbal and nonverbal—that may seem somehow offensive. If you're not sure if a young person meant to insult you, then it's likely that he or she did not, because this bold generation does not mince words. Beyond this, it takes effort to learn new technologies by which messages are sent. In my own example, hindsight taught me that when someone sends a text that reads "we have to start at 9 AM," it is wise to clarify the correct *arrival* time.

As another example, when a church attendee says, "This church isn't doing anything to help the poor," rather than being defensive, church leaders should inquire about the generalization. Likely, as stated previously, the young person is unaware of what resources the church really is investing in benevolent activities. It's important to remain calm and make sure the conversation is a two-way street. Perhaps the young adult has ideas about how to improve the church's effectiveness in this area of ministry and likely would passionately work toward the cause. If so, utilize that energy! What the individual needs is to be heard and to see his or her ideas and efforts flourish within the community.

TECHNOLOGY'S PLACE

Older individuals who are particularly tech-savvy may be able to bridge the gap by starting online blogs, launching YouTube channels, or connecting through other forms of social media. These efforts can supplement interpersonal activity, but remember that they don't effectively substitute person-to-person interaction. For others seeking to find a way to visit without the interference of devices, negotiations may be successful—for example, an hour of immersion into technology on the part of the older person might be exchanged for an hour of silenced devices on the part of the younger. Such bartering may seem to go a step too far, but considering some of the extreme challenges sweeping through the lives of today's youth, such as those mentioned in chapter 1, what distance is too far to answer a cry for help? Striking a bargain could be merely one more way of engaging in the vital process of getting to know a Millennial.

STOP SAYING, "ALL I CAN DO IS PRAY"

Prayer is the first step a mentor should take. Whenever possible, long before an interpersonal connection begins, it should be bathed in prayer. If you are considering mentoring, trust that God will bring you the person who will be particularly receptive to the type of wisdom you have to impart. Petition God to prepare the heart of the individual or group of individuals you'll become involved with. Ask Him to make you ready as well for the friendship that will be brought into your world. As you begin to establish relationships, pray for individuals specifically. Pay attention when they tell you details about their lives—or notice when they refuse to share information with you at all. Make any subject they're willing to open up about a matter of prayer, and for those who are particularly withdrawn, ask God to mend their wounds so that they will feel safe enough to enter the friendship process. Beyond this, ask God for His wisdom in all things, so that you'll always have the right words.

Create in me a clean heart, O God; and renew a right spirit within me. (Psalms 51:10)

The mouth of the righteous speaketh wisdom, and his tongue talketh of judgment. (Psalms 37:30)

BALANCE TRUTH WITH LOVE

We discussed Keith and Melody Green's radical, sold-out approach to reaching the lost earlier in this chapter. Not everybody is able to minister in the same manner as they did, nor is everybody called to do so. However, when God moves, people who wholeheartedly follow His direction often end up doing quirky, unusual things that would not work under any other circumstance, but that work strangely well in that specific time and setting. Green was such a radical that some found him to be offensive at times. (Does this remind you of the Millennial crowd?) Regardless, his motivator was love and, in a few short years, he and his wife fostered a ministry that far outlasted his lifetime. Like so many other subjects discussed in this book, what caused his ministry to thrive was the matter of his heart, where he found a balance of both love and truth.

Love without truth becomes a mere emotion, which for some translates to being vulnerable and ungrounded. On the other hand, truth without love is legalism and only draws a small crowd at best. For lives to change, love must be so strong that it is able to withstand the application of truth. When we fervently seek to apply both, lasting benefits are set into motion.

Many confuse this important concept where Christianity is concerned, and with devastating results: Either religion becomes love with no basis of truth or it becomes truth with no basis of love. Our youth of today are asking to be shown how to live out the balance between these two.

LOOK FOR THE CLUES BEHIND THE COMPLAINT

DISCIPLESHIP

For many, getting a request to disciple a younger person uncovers inhibitions grounded in their own self-uncertainty. Those who aren't theologians may be tempted to decline, assuming they have nothing to offer. However, Millennials themselves clarify what they are petitioning when they make this invitation: "Discipleship should begin and grow like any friendship. 'It's not complicated' explains one young husband and dad. 'Just spend time with us. Addressing issues and learning more will come with the relationship, just like it does with God. The more we know Him, the more we grow in Him.'"[260] The request for being discipled is much like that of being mentored, but with scriptural discovery as the basis for the interaction.

CLUMPING "THE CHURCH" WITH "THE CHURCH'S PEOPLE"

Furthermore, we've well established by now that many complaints the younger generations have toward the church are not always intended to extend to the *individuals* within the church. Many frustrations with the religious institution are often taken personally by those who attend, but this is a different issue. Millennial Caitlin Meadows of *Artios* magazine clarifies: "While…Millennials may not possess a love for *attending* church, I argue that my generation does love *the Church*. In other words, we love the body of Christ. And we are committed to it."[261] Those individuals who meet within the walls of the church are those who are actually being invited, *by our youth*, to join them in creating a far-reaching, worldwide community that extends the gospel of Jesus Christ. These are two very different statements being made by the same group of people. Granted, both messages use similar *words*; but it is vital that we recognize the distinction between each of these messages and react accordingly.

UNIFIED CHURCH

Scripture is full of examples of churches riddled with conflict, or of people making mistakes within the Body—for example, 1 Corinthians 5, 6:1– 11, 14:26–40; Galatians 1:6–10; Colossians 2:4–23; 2 Thessalonians 3:6–15; and Titus 3:9–11. While young people may be less seasoned, they certainly aren't naïve. They are well aware that there are flawed people within the church. However, it is essential for those who are representing your church to be sincere. It is off-putting to visitors to be welcomed with warmth by someone at church, only to have that same person snub them throughout the rest of the week in other places within the community.

The crux of this issue is, as stated previously, a matter of the heart. Our modern young adults want to invest their efforts with groups of people who they feel are transparent and *endeavor* to do the right thing. Everybody has made mistakes; a unified church must be scripturally founded and interested in putting God's will first. This doesn't mean that the Millennial expects everyone in a church to be perfect at all times, only that churchgoers should be unified in their scriptural integrity and in their sincere willingness to be the best representation of Christ that they can.

IMAGINE IF...

Imagine what could happen if the generation gap narrowed, Millennials began to experience revival as the Body of Christ activated in a visible way throughout the earth, and we finally realized the promise made in Scripture: "And it shall come to pass afterward, that I will pour out my spirit upon all flesh; and your sons and your daughters shall prophesy, your old men shall dream dreams, your young men shall see visions" (Joel 2:28). The world is primed for such a movement, and a new perspective on each of Millennials' attributes will yield a strength that can be channeled to make this powerful, young generation a force for good: an indispensable, community-driven, motivated, and active dynamism behind the passionate future church.

In March of 2018, in an interview wherein several Millennials discussed their reasons for leaving the church, Grant Skeldon asked a powerful question: "Why is the most cause-oriented generation in the world not connecting with the most cause-oriented organization in the world: the church?"[262]

This book has gone to great lengths to answer that question, and likewise to outline what can be done to remedy the situation. So now, I will ask the reader another question, one that serves as an *extension* to Skeldon's regarding the church and Millennials: What will happen when this connection finally takes place and these two forces unite?

8

NOW, A WORD TO
THE MILLENNIALS

DEAR MILLENNIAL,

I hope that by this point in the book you have gained confidence in the intentions of this work and its regard of every member of the young generation. The motivation has been to narrow the existing societal/age gaps and dispel many of the stereotypes that exist about you by helping individuals of different circumstances and backgrounds understand each other. Throughout this work, my goal has been to bring to light the common ground between generations and raise the potential for bridges to be rebuilt.

While the great bulk of this work has been dedicated to helping members of the older generations develop a healthy perception of Millennials, it would be delivered without balance if not presented with a segment devoted, in turn, to helping you understand the older generations. After all, meeting in the middle is only fair. Just as the case has been made throughout the pages of this book for the origin of your worldview, that of older generations was likewise forged by their own season of fire, which thus contributed to their point of view on various life issues. Furthermore, every older-aged person who has taken the time to read up to this point has likely done so in an effort to better understand, minister to, and connect with you. In consideration of this investment on their part, I ask that you read on with a humble heart and an open mind as I attempt to relay to you some more information that may help you on your journey.

You Are Not the Worst Generation

I do not believe the negative statements about your generation are true; I don't think you are selfish, entitled, lazy, or narcissistic, or that you want to lead without working your way up. These are generalizations and, while each age group probably includes some who fit these unbecoming profiles, most Millennials are simply misunderstood. The youthful zeal displayed by every generation (currently yours), combined with the sheer speed with which you make decisions and communicate, is likely a large contributing factor to these stereotypes. The irony is that you, yourselves, have repeatedly asked for help in channeling your fervor constructively by requesting a setting wherein you can direct these energies toward community involvement. This indicates your desire to connect on a personal level. Furthermore, your request for mentorship shows that you're willing to be lovingly critiqued and taught.

You can find both community and mentorship in a church family, and that is likewise a setting where you can organically break out of negative, age-related generalizations by fostering relationships with people, learning from those who have the advantage of experience, and by finding a way to make a vital contribution that reaches farther into the world than you can on your own. Sadly, as we've mentioned often throughout this book, many of you are leaving the church, and by doing so are walking away from the circumstances that can best provide the very answer to their desires and requests.

ABOUT COMMUNITY

The desire to belong to a community isn't unique to your generation. In fact, it's been a human need since Adam and Eve were created. God's original intention for mankind was to exist in the Garden of Eden, a serene setting wherein people were given continual access to each other and to God Himself. Genesis 2 describes this place as having four rivers that flowed through it, as being endowed with such precious substances as gold and onyx, and as being a place where man and woman wouldn't have to work. In the Garden, mankind's needs would be provided. In the beginning, this was our destiny. Unfortunately, this utopian setting was forever tainted when God's orders were disobeyed. Perhaps this is why each of us, deep inside, yearns for such a situation. C. S. Lewis said: "If we find ourselves with a desire that nothing in this world can satisfy, the most probable explanation is that we were made for another world."[263] There is a great amount of wisdom in this.

The fact that God's original objective for mankind shifted with the Fall of Man doesn't mean that we're any less hardwired for community. Likewise, our ability to plug into and contribute to a group of other individuals is still essential to fulfillment. When you ask someone in the older generation to help you thrive, you're on the right track. However, when you become frustrated and leave the church (thus foregoing a great opportunity to be involved in the type of fellowship you're seeking), you're forgetting an important truth—on that, C. S. Lewis commented on as well: "If you think of this world as a place simply intended for our happiness, you find it quite intolerable: think of it as a place for correction and training and it's not so bad."[264]

Often we spend our childhoods imagining adult life to be a certain way (whether this vision is shaped by our own fancies, false representation on the part of well-meaning parents and teachers, or some other factor). When we finally reach adulthood, we find that the world is every bit as flawed as we dreaded. The disappointment that often follows can result in a youthful zeal that motivates us to want to change the world. This is a powerful driving force that you should carefully direct into constructive areas without becoming depressed or hopeless because of the disillusionment that accompanies coming of age. Understand that the current setting is a mere preliminary to the eternal destination that God has in mind for us, and our human needs and longings are designed to drive us to that place. You are dissatisfied because you are hardwired to be somewhere else, and your journey toward that destination is not over:

> He will swallow up death in victory; and the Lord God will wipe away tears from off all faces, and the rebuke of His people shall He take away from off all the earth; for the Lord hath spoken it. And it shall be said in that day: "Lo, this is our God; we have waited for Him; we will be glad and rejoice in His salvation." (Isaiah 25:8–9)

The desires in the heart of every person to live in a community of beauty, peace, and love will be met on that day when we are reunited in heaven with our Lord. We will share in His triumph over death and we will no longer be rebuked or out of place; we will have a home where we truly *belong forever*. We will celebrate that our wait for that perfect day is over, and we will dwell with our God in the ultimate community that will be heaven. Until then, we live in a world that is imperfect, and the yearning for our final intended destination aches inside each of us.

Many members of your own generation have stated that young people don't expect church members to be perfect, only transparent and sincere. This is a noble and understandable stipulation. However, as we've touched upon throughout the book, often, what appears to be a lack of action or earnestness on the part of religious institutions can be a breakdown of communication. Just as I encouraged members of the older generation to engage in two-way dialogue, I entreat you to do the same. The fact that your age group is so outspoken about the desire to see the church revolutionize and become active in all parts of the world—both geographically and socioculturally—serves as evidence that your desires intertwine with the thread of God's plan for His Church. This said, I'll move on to the next vital point I want to share with you.

WE NEED YOU

In a previous chapter, we discussed the revolutionary ministry of Keith Green. While he lived during a different era, he was, like you, a young adult when his fiery lyrics caught the attention of the church. What was he frustrated with? Similar elements to the grievances that your age group has cited: As stated regarding the man before, his protests were related to a complacent, hypocritical body of people who call themselves believers but are not compelled to action. Does this sound like a familiar complaint to you?

Just last Sunday, I sat in my home church, listening to a sermon preached by the fervent, dedicated man who pastors our small body of believers. Pondering that I would soon be writing this segment of these pages specifically to Millennials, a Scripture that I've heard and read countless times struck me in a new light:

Not every one that saith unto Me, "Lord, Lord," shall enter into the Kingdom of Heaven, but he that doeth the will of My Father who is in Heaven. Many will say to Me in that Day, "Lord,

Lord, have we not prophesied in Thy name, and in Thy name have cast out devils, and in Thy name done many wonderful works?" And then will I profess unto them, "I never knew you: depart from Me, ye that work iniquity." (Matthew 7:21–23)

Our preacher went on to elaborate on the word "iniquity," explaining that it is more than obstinate behavior toward God; it also refers to those who do not live in accordance with His will. This passage does not refer to the sinners who outwardly rebel against God and disregard His law; rather, it refers to those who busy themselves with what they perceive to be *God's work*, and yet miss the whole relationship aspect of serving Him. What a sad reality to think of those who go about their daily lives imagining that they are righteous in the sight of God's eyes, but who completely miss the mark.

While I had previously been aware of the passage's meaning in this regard, a new thought occurred to me: This is one area where your generation can be vital in the church. This Scripture has a similar ring to many of the statements that you've made regarding passion, relationship, and even hypocrisy within modern religious institution. You've already proven you're bold enough to speak out against pretense, lack of activism, and other issues that you see. Communication must be made with love and with an open mind to the guidance of older, more experienced believers, but your willingness to speak the truth on these matters *could very well launch the next revival of the church.*

Instead of pointing out the problems as you leave, we need you to stay and be part of the solution.

ON COMMUNICATION AND CHANGE

As previously stated, much of the miscommunication between you and members of the older generation is because you have differing points of view on similar issues. Worth mentioning here is the contrast between the young adult's aversion to institutions and the security an older person finds in them. Most members of our older generation were profoundly impacted in one way or another by the events of the Great Depression. This was a time of extreme poverty, scarcity of resources, and suffering on every level. Families struggled with homelessness, starvation, a lack of medicines available for illnesses, and an overreaching sense of powerlessness over the situation. I know of several people who recall spending days as young children working in the sun (if they were fortunate enough to find work) and who were still sent to bed hungry despite the family's labors. Many older folks, as mentioned earlier, found that such woeful circumstances caused families to draw closer to one another as they worked as a team for survival, and the lack of every type of resource left them with nowhere to turn but to God, which strengthened their faith.

The aftermath of these events created a domino effect that was devastating in many ways. However, those who lives through that difficult time determined to prevent anything similar from occurring in the future. This resolve indirectly contributed to the establishment of labor laws and employee advocates, increased the availability of education, and led to the creation of public works programs such as our modern Social Security system and clearer public policy regarding child welfare. These revolutions in our political economy over the last century directly benefitted our older generation. Rules, procedures, and even some institutions, birthed out of an effort to create a safer economic and political infrastructure for future generations, became a "safety net" for many. Furthermore, through this desolate period of time, families clung to continue traditions that had been ingrained within their sentiment and faith. While the younger collective is suspicious and distrusting of institutions and sometimes sees tradition as a waste of time or resources, those are significantly close to an older person's heart.

Members of our oldest generations are people who stockpiled items such as restaurant "to go" containers, threadbare towels, and bread twist ties because they knew they could find a use for those items later and did not dare waste any type of resource. They took the time to darn a hole-ridden sock instead of throwing it out. As profoundly as technology has influenced *your* worldview, it may help you to understand that starvation, poverty, and the general struggles of life's cruelty deeply reflects in theirs. This said, naturally, anytime people have come to a place where they feel at peace, asking them to make changes can result in resistance. This is often more than mere stubbornness; it is like asking people to give up something that makes them secure.

Furthermore, there is a deep-seeded thread of patriotism in our older collective, and for good reason. The freedoms we enjoy today were paid for by these and preceding generations, and they take this matter seriously. Thus, anytime a proposed change reflects that of separation of church and state or of removing icons of time-honored American heritage from religious institutions, be prepared for an emotional response. Blogger Jordan Rimmer stated:

> Older generations are patriotic. For them, the country is the institution to which we all owe loyalty.... Many of them personally sacrificed either in military service or as their family members fought in wars. They grew up pledging allegiance to the flag... This is why they don't want you moving the flag out of their sanctuary. For them it is not just a move to separate church and state. It is an anti-American statement.[265]

Finally, I want to say this: In the same way that a few generalizations have been used to unjustly label your entire generation, many older folks are judged quickly as being unfair, unreasonable, or stuck in their ways. Similarly, these tags are often inaccurate. As we've looked at earlier, many people who are progressed in years don't know exactly how to relate to the modern Millennial state of circumstances, but this doesn't mean they aren't interested in helping you. Some may not instantly know how to relate or be supportive, but as a Millennial who passionately wants to network with others, surely you can see the importance of patiently working through this.

ON THE MATTER OF TRUTH

Young adults have repeatedly stated that they're frustrated that they don't believe the church is tackling tough issues. As previously explained, many shy away from controversial subjects in an effort to stick to the primary reason that the church exists: telling the world that Jesus loves them and that He died for them. However, you are correct about something: once people make the decision to follow Christ they must "walk the walk" during their remaining years. For this reason, it's necessary to find answers to life's difficult questions. What you are asking for is scriptural: you want to be taken off the "milk" and given the "meat" of God's Word:

> I have fed you with milk and not with meat; for hitherto ye were not able to bear it, neither yet now are ye able. (1 Corinthians 3:2)

> For at the time when ye ought to be teachers, ye have need that one teach you again the first principles of the oracles of God, and have become such as have the need of milk, and not strong meat. (Hebrews 5:12)

When people in the older generation leave their comfort zone to provide coaching in a manner they believe is scriptural, subsequent conversations must be handled gently. Defensiveness will likely send the message that you don't want to be mentored or are unteachable. Remember that sometimes, there are growing pains when we get what we've asked for.

When I was very little—when Baby Boomers were in *their* early adulthood—I remember seeing a commercial for a 1976 Toyota with the slogan: "You asked for it, you got it!"[266] This may very well be how the same generation responds to your request for definite lines to be drawn on issues of morality. I encourage all parties to handle these conversations in love as you sort through Scripture together. It is likely that ministers who step out on a limb to speak on tough issues does so either in response to requests from congregants or because they feel that God has prompted them to do so. After all, someone interested in winning a popularity contest would certainly avoid controversial issues. For this reason, when your request for truth is met with discussion, please respond with an open mind. When you take your concerns to church leadership, this is precisely the attitude you'll hope to be met with. Constructive conversation is a two-way street.

I also encourage you to be cautious with the matter of truth. As explained earlier in the book, philosophical approaches to both the notion of truth and of religion have morphed significantly over the centuries—and more quickly over the past several decades. Recall, however, statements made about the necessity of reality hinging on a moral constant. If there are no ethics or concrete realities by which truth is mounted and people custom-design their own, we're left with a society where very few chunks of *actual, real certainty* exist. The result is a population whose individual points of view (essentially, personal opinions) are spoken as though they're fact. And, sadly, if and when those convinced of their position begin to teach others, a group of people are misled. In your search for absolute truth, I implore you to require that all concepts you decide to follow line up with Scripture.

DISENGAGE FROM LINGUAL SABOTAGE

When we make a request from others, it's vital to understand *what* we're asking *for*. As discussed previously, sometimes our modern language is skewed, impeding communication. Recall how such words as "identity" and "tolerance" fuel an undertone of division. Understand the request you're making when you use those or similar words. For example, if you're at peace with "agreeing to disagree" with others, tolerance becomes the appropriate petition. However, this doesn't guarantee that another individual will agree with you; nor does it insinuate a lack of friendship of those who don't see things your way. If, on the other hand, what you are seeking is love and unconditional acceptance, inquire accordingly. If unequivocal agreement is the goal, that is yet a separate conversation, one in which the word "tolerance" will only cause friction. This isn't the only example of lingual sabotage occurring in our modern society. I encourage you to analyze your communication and be on guard for the many opportunities for sabotage that exist within modern dialogue.

THE WORLD MOVES FASTER EVERY DAY

It seems as though anyone, when asked these days, will heartily agree that the pace at which the world moves seems to perpetually pick up speed. The stride at which communication, technology, human interaction, and even practical activities such as cooking has increased dramatically. A perfect illustration of this is the English word "hodiernal," derived from the mid-seventeenth-century Latin word *hodiernus*. The word's original root meant "today,"[267] but the definition evolved to mean "relating to the present day"[268] or, more specifically, it was used to describe anything pertaining to the current moment in time. Ironically, this word has become completely outdated. Time literally moved so quickly that a word embodying what it means to be contemporary and up-to-date became archaic. This is how fast our world is spinning.

For you, life has always been presented at top speed and members of your age group have unquestioningly adapted. However, the older percentage of our population is still reeling. They remember a time before technology, when the hours of the day moved at a slower pace and conversation was delivered in unhurried, steady slices, face to face, and not in two lines or less via a quick text. For subsequent generations born and raised in the digital age, this gap may be less profound. However, for this moment, the wedge imposed by this divide requires patience from both age groups for successful relationships.

WHAT ARE YOUR DREAMS?

While the pace of our society continues to increase, the issues our young adults face likewise are more convoluted. I believe individuals gradually drift farther from the simplicity of dreaming about personal calling, destiny, and legacy as a result of being spread too thin. Your generation's propensity to get involved in activism shows that there is a visionary streak motivating you. So, the question becomes this: What will you do with this valuable attribute? By the way, this crossroad is not unique to your generation. In fact, Scripture assures us that if we surrender our lives to God's will, His purpose will be manifested through us:

> Therefore, my beloved, as ye have always obeyed, not only in my presence, but now much more in my absence, work out your own salvation with fear and trembling. For it is God who worketh in you, both to will and to do of his good pleasure. (Philippians 2:12–13)

When considering your dreams, don't make the mistake of thinking that a life of grandeur is a fulfilling one. One thing your generation has been accused of is having unrealistically high expectations about your career, home life, financial status, and more. While we've previously addressed those issues, one additional perspective should be emphasized: Even those who achieve their loftiest aspirations are often, in the end, still unhappy. Like so many other circumstances in life, contentment can be misrepresented as material wealth, status, or other desirable situations. Regardless of whether the enviable person who has in fact achieved wealth, status, and more has achieved satisfaction, it is a common mistake for onlookers to confuse outward displays of triumph with *inner success*. These are very different from each other, and often one comes without the other.

Recall my story of playing tic-tac-toe with Grandpa Fuller. During the time I him before he retired, he was a locksmith and a school janitor. Certainly, these are honorable professions, and Grandpa Fuller had a good work ethic, but his financial situation was a humble one. However, he was one of the most content and fulfilled individuals that I knew. This is because he lived his life in a way that focused on purpose, destiny, and the inner peace that comes from knowing that one is living according to the will of God. A life invested in this way is one that becomes enviable in a manner that money cannot purchase. Likewise, it is what attracts others to join you.

> Fret not about anything, but in everything, by prayer and supplication with thanksgiving, let your requests be made known unto God. And the peace of God, which passeth all understanding, shall keep your hearts and minds through Jesus Christ. (Philippians 4:6–7)

Everybody wants to be or do something important. After all, there is only so much time allotted to one lifespan and no one wants to waste it. For many, being "lost in the crowd" is a very real concern. We strive for individuality and uniqueness. This drives some of us to extremes as we attempt to fabricate something spectacular about ourselves. For others, the lack of strategy for overcoming this vulnerability contributes to low self-esteem (and, likely stems *from* low self-esteem as well). Others resort to overachieving, while still others foster destructive behaviors as an aversion to the topic altogether. The irony of this point is that as we each respond uniquely to this common insecurity, our varied reactions *prove* how distinctive we all are. And yet, in the eyes of our Creator, we have each been given individual attention since before birth:

> Thus says the Lord, your Redeemer, who formed you from the womb: "I am the Lord, who made all things, who alone stretched out the heavens, who spread out the earth by myself." (Isaiah 44:24)

> Upon you I have leaned from before my birth; you are he who took me from my mother's womb. My praise is continually of you. (Psalm 71:6)

In a world that distracts us relentlessly, I assert that you have been robbed of the opportunity to dream your destiny. I encourage each of you to think about the fact that you were born with a purpose and that God has a plan for your life. You have asked for this repeatedly—whether you realize it or not—through your frequent requests of community interaction. Without a sense of destiny and purpose, it is likely that you'll continue to feel lost and disconnected from others.

A good place to start in this search is with the Creator who hardwired you with such desires in the first place. I ask that you to lay aside your frustrations with religion and make a sincere attempt to reconnect with the One who should be at the center of it: God the Father, God the Son, and God the Holy Spirit. This may also be a nice time to reconnect with nature, as leaving the world of electronics behind can make it easier to hear God's voice. (In addition, you might get a greatly needed break!) Hike a waterfall trail, go to the park and walk barefoot in the grass, or, if you're not an outdoor person, sit in a quiet place inside somewhere peaceful. Find some undistracted time to spend prayerfully soul-searching as you consider the reason God placed you where you are. Remember the four essential questions noted by Ravi Zacharias regarding the moment that Jesus changed His life:

Origin: where do I come from?
Meaning: what gives life meaning?
Morality: how do I differentiate between good and bad?
Destiny: what happens to human beings when they die?[269]

As noted previously, these questions have to be "correspondingly true…and [when it is] all put together, it has to cohere."[270] When you search your soul and arrive at the answers to these questions, you'll likely have a similar revelation to that of Zacharias. When Jesus changes your life, He doesn't merely change what you do; He changes *what you want to do* (with your future).[271] Allowing God to work in your life will activate your dream, unleashing your destiny.

REGARDING THE CHURCH'S CHARITY

The time we spend on this subject will be abbreviated since we covered it earlier at greater length. However, in speaking directly to the Millennial generation, my desire is to reiterate that there is often a communication gap between church government and church congregants. Likewise, it is already been established that the Scriptural stance on giving places emphasis on anonymity. If you're attending a church and can't see the fruits of charitable giving, it doesn't mean that it's not taking place. I implore you to inquire with a humble heart before jumping to any conclusions—and *certainly* before you take such action as leaving the church. Furthermore, if you were to attend a church that continually boasted of its giving, you may find this off-putting in the long-term, considering there might be ulterior motives behind the generosity.

There are many ways of inquiring about church finances, although each institution has different protocol. Often, these matters are addressed at business meetings. While those who aren't members might not be allowed to comment or vote, it is likely that you are invited to sit in and listen. If you would like to be more involved than this, consider taking steps toward becoming a member.

On Leadership

Leadership is another topic that has been previously discussed and thus will be truncated here. Many churches have extensive policies (for good reason) about what it takes to qualify to volunteer in various positions. This may seem frustrating to a young adult who is enthusiastic and wants to jump right in! However, most church bylaws have been written out of circumstances that necessitate such guidelines. Certainly, those in church government now will eventually have to relinquish the responsibility to the upcoming generation, and your opportunity to become involved must be realized. But, be prepared for a process of training and mentorship that begins with small tasks and grows from there.

Individuals must go through much seasoning before they're admitted to leadership. While a slow start may seem agonizing at first, the long-term picture may be that you will eventually grow to appreciate the institution's steadier approach to taking on new workers. After all, a church that places any and all volunteers in top leadership, financial, or childcare positions, without an extensive screening, mentorship, and approval process may employ your efforts more quickly, but it also might strike you as careless. Keep an open mind and patience mind as you attempt to enter the arena of ministerial work.

Furthermore, religious institutions must consider many qualifications—such as education (if applicable), experience, or Bible knowledge—as they promote workers from one position to another. Other qualifications are more ambiguous, such as accountability and even a person's age. (For example, I once wanted to teach a Wednesday night class to preteens, but because I was a teen myself, the director told me it wouldn't be a good idea. She said that while I was *mature and capable enough* to handle the job, she was concerned that I was too close in age to those I would be teaching and thus would not obtain their respect/attention. I was then allowed to serve a younger class.)

Many churches have additional varying parameters regarding what they ask of those in leadership. Some require those who serve to sign personal conduct agreements, which specify abstinence from such activities as attending movies with certain ratings, using tobacco or alcohol products, engaging in drug abuse or sexual immorality, or participating in other types of conduct that isn't appropriate for church leaders. Once you take on a role as a leader, you may find that you are observed under a new level of scrutiny. This is fairly common and is simply how church leadership attempts to regulate the conduct of their leaders—a practice fortified by the following passage: "For unto whomsoever much is given, of him shall much be required; and to whom men have committed much, of him they will ask the more" (Luke 12:48).

From the outside looking in, many people assume that serving in leadership is glamorous or prestigious, but accountability and responsibility come with this function; those who serve must begin with humility and have a willingness to be mentored. A delay of serving in smaller capacities may disappoint enthusiastic young adults, but the additional time will help season the up-and-comer for eventually taking on the responsibilities of leadership.

Consider the insight offered by Jordan Rimmer of the Pittsburg Theological Seminary in a recent blog regarding the plight of many modern young ministers: "There are an increasing number of millennials who did not grow up in church and are now becoming pastors. Many of them are struggling in ministry because they do not understand the older generations."[272] In this commentary, Rimmer discusses the fact that older people are not technology oriented and they can be resistant to change. He points out how the generation gap can manifest within the church:

> Some of [the older folks] worked for the same company their whole lives. They live in the same home they grew up in. Now they are seeing their kids and grandkids move away to follow a new job every couple of years. In all of this change, the one thing that has stayed the same is the church. It has been their anchor. That is why they sometimes react strongly to changes in the church.[273]

In the long run, a time of preparation will benefit your ministry and provide a smoother transition for affected members of all generations. When you are redirected to help with tasks that seem less grand than what you initially wanted to do, try not to see this as a type of rejection. Instead, consider it for what it likely is: You're being initiated into a ministry that will surely become a long-lasting focus of your life.

BELONGING GOES BOTH WAYS

Many members of the young generation have made bold statements about church members—or entire religious institutions—coming off as "fake." While it is true that there are disingenuous people within the church, fraudulent people can be found in nearly every setting of society.

As previously stated, for many young people, going to church is "no longer the cool thing to do."[274] Bearing this in mind, it is unlikely that every church you visit will be filled with people who are insincere. In fact, it is highly probable that because of religion's decreasing popularity, a large percentage of those who remain are there for honest reasons. So why does it seem that churches are so filled with "fake" people?

The cause may stem from the nobility of the church's mission. What I mean is this: Church *should* be the one place in the world where honest, godly, self-sacrificing individuals gather and where the lost can find safe harbor from the cruelties of the world. Within the Body of Christ, we should be safe to show our vulnerabilities and shortcomings without fear of being stabbed in the back or double-crossed. Thus, when a hypocritical person is detected within what should be a tightly interwoven network of godly people, internal alarms sound so loudly that they have the potential to cause others to retreat completely.

However, as noted earlier, insincere people are found within every subset of culture. Physically walking into a sanctuary and sitting upon a pew does not guarantee the condition of one's heart. With this said, I implore you to get to as many people as you can in your local church; don't judge the entire group by your opinion of a few individuals. This is a reversed version of many requests made by the Millennial generation to the rest of society: You have asked for personal relationships and resist generalizations made about your generation based on the behaviors of a small percentage of you. Church can provide the very community involvement you've requested. I highly recommend that you get to know individuals within the church on a personal basis and surround yourself with those who don't strike you as feigning their faith.

Additionally, when visiting a church, please try to get to know people before you assume they've divided into cliques. This is a common accusation made toward members of churches—it's not exclusive to your generation at all. However, often the situation is similar to that of the accusation of churchgoers being insincere. Because the Body of

Christ *should* be one large group without division, the appearance of subfactions within a congregation has the potential to set off internal alarms that send people packing. If you sense cliquishness or an exclusive attitude from church members, make sure before you move on that you're not misunderstanding the situation. Again, encircle yourself with people who are welcoming and conversational, while dedicating some time to see what develops with the congregation as a whole.

Many churches have greeters who stand inside the door and shake hands with visitors. However, many members are unsure of how to approach the newcomers once they've made it past this point. I can tell you this firsthand, because it is often my dilemma: Churchgoers want to welcome the visitors, yet are unsure of how much attention they're prepared for. How much is too much? How little is too little? Would they enjoy an exuberant handshake or are they shy, preferring to quietly slip in and out of the service until they feel more comfortable? In my own experience (here's a moment of transparency), I usually offer an awkward, timid greeting, wherein I attempt to let visitors know we're glad they've arrived without sending a signal that they can expect to be singled out every time they enter the church building. In truth, it's a greeting that some may perceive as "fake," but it comes from a place of honesty. Persevering past the initial moments of awkwardness as we get to know each other likely proves worthwhile.

ANSWER THIS QUESTION

When it comes to the issue of church attendance, many say it is vital to being a Christian, while others say that it isn't. Some cite the following to fortify the case for attending church:

> And let us consider one another to provoke unto love and to good works, not forsaking the assembling of ourselves together,

as is the manner of some, but exhorting one another, and so much more as ye see the Day approaching. (Hebrews 10:24–25)

While this doesn't say we lose salvation if we aren't in church on Sunday, it relays an important nuance that's often overlooked: By gathering with other Christians, we "provoke" each other to do loving and good acts. Your generation has made many outspoken assertions about your need to see the Body of Christ doing more good in the world. By attending church, we should be prompting each other toward activism. We are instructed to encourage each other to do the right thing, because there is strength in numbers.

However, each person who enters a church must be able to answer these questions: Why am I here? What did I expect to gain by entering this building? What am I looking for? Many people don't think to ask these questions before they enter a religious institution, and this uncertainty is worsened by the awkwardness of realizing a person has entered a room filled with strangers. In a secular setting such as a coffee shop or library, people can simply busy themselves privately to stave off their discomfort, but church activities depend on participation, forcing reluctant spectators to engage.

At this point, many may privately wish that the answer to these questions would magically manifest to them inwardly, bestowing them with a sense of purpose for why they have subjected themselves to such a moment of awkwardness. Occasionally, just such an answer is internally manifested, resulting in a dynamic testimony of transcendent, revealed purpose that strikes the individual who wandered into a church building uncertain of the reason, and whose life was majestically transformed by God on that day as a result. But for many others, that moment of social ungainliness becomes the primary takeaway from the church experience.

Some churches are settings where visitors are readily embraced by attendees who welcome them in love and ensure them that it's a place of belonging. However, this doesn't mean that the visitors are immediately *comfortable*. People can take some control over the outcome of this experience by having answers to these questions in advance. For example, young adults have stated repeatedly that they're not looking for a "social club," but for biblical teaching and religious transcendence. Upon entering a sanctuary and feeling like the odd person out, recalling this contrast of desires can help people keep their mission in focus until they've gotten to know fellow churchgoers enough to *feel* a sense of belonging.

WHERE IS YOUR PAIN?

It's safe to say that everybody who lives on planet earth has had negative experiences, bad memories, and trials to overcome. This is part of the human experience, with no exceptions. However, many wise people say that our pain is what makes us stronger. It has been stated throughout the book that persevering through obstacles brings valuable experience and patience. Likewise, it is well established that young adults want to change the world. So I ask you: Where is your pain?

I realize this is an intrusive question, but where your hurt is located is where you likewise can be an effective advocate for righteousness. Your generation repeatedly shows a passionate motivation to make the world a better place for those who are suffering. And likely, those areas where you yourself have anguished are the places where you're best equipped to make a difference for others. Scripture tells us that when God has delivered us from our own troubles, He can use that situation to glorify Him. Beyond this, we can draw a metaphorical "road map" to help and encourage others: "Offer unto God thanksgiving, and pay thy vows unto the Most High, and call upon Me in the day of trouble; I will deliver thee, and thou shalt glorify Me" (Psalms 50:14–15).

COME BACK TO CHURCH

Millennial Derek Rishmawy, in his article entitled "The Church Failed Millennials, Just Not in the Way You Think It Did," explains his transformation from frustrated Millennial on his way out the church door to enthusiastic attendee. The key? Personal investment. Rishmawy recounts his story of complaining to an older person about various grievances he had against the modern religious institution when the person he was talking to challenged him by asking him if he had been praying about it. This was a new idea to him, as he had always presumed that the organization was there to pray for *him*, not vice versa. Reversing that concept set him on a new course.

> By praying for it and serving it, I began to *love* it like I never really had before. Instead of viewing it through the non-committal, arm's distance, American, semi-apathy I had settled into, I saw its weaknesses and failures in the stark, glaring light of love. The thing about that love, though, is that it didn't drive me away, but drew me deeper in. I came to the point where walking away from it wasn't even an option.[275]

Rishmawy also acknowledges that the longer he invested his own efforts and prayer into the church, the more he realized that some of his earlier judgment had been more a byproduct of "youth and haste"[276] than of the actions of the Body itself: "I began to see all of the wonderful works Jesus was working in his Bride that I simply been too jaded and frustrated to notice before."[277] The essential challenge Rishmawy asserts is this: Before you walk out, citing a list of shortcomings and exasperations as your reason, will you commit to pray for the church and serve there?

I encourage each young adult who has read this book to make an effort to see your grievances with the Body of Christ with a new perspective based on some of the insights you've gained. Likewise, I admonish members of the older generations to adopt a new outlook toward the upcoming generations. Allow me to encourage individuals of all ages to drop your defenses and communicate openly and with patience. Inventory your strengths and talents—even your hurts, and find where these attributes channel together to establish a sense of purpose…and then *dream it*. Don't let the world rob you of your true identity, destiny, or legacy. And finally, I encourage you to intertwine this newfound personal momentum with the vision God has for His Bride.

TO THE MILLENNIAL, I SAY:

You have repeatedly requested relationship and mentorship, and right now, your numbers within the church are dwindling, meaning that you have limitless access to numerous seasoned adults who are *waiting for you.*

You are vocal, bold, and not easily intimidated. You want to be involved in leadership, and the future of the church needs a generation of people who are willing to speak out on tough issues, regardless of whether the mainstream crowd finds such statements palatable. Our modern church needs outspoken advocates for truth—advocates *just like you.*

You continually show your motivation toward activism because you care about others and you want to improve the world in a way that outlasts your life. The community that is the church wants to give you a place where your passions and efforts can make a difference that outlasts this lifetime. The result can be a legacy that is eternal *because of you.*

You want a community, and many of the shortcomings you have cited with religious organizations have validity. However, your passion—ignited under the guidance, encouragement, relationship, and mentorship of church elders—could be the key to revolutionizing that institution, fueling the next revival that stretches to the farthest corners of the planet. There is *only one you*, and *only you* can perform exclusively the function that God has for you within His Church. The role that you can play in the Body of Christ is *unique to you.*

Come back to church; we need *you.*

NOTES

1. Serafino, Jay. "New Guidelines Redefine Birth Years for Millennials, Gen-X, and 'Post-Millennials'." *Mental Floss Online*. March 1, 2018. http://mentalfloss.com/article/533632/new-guidelines-redefine-birth-years-millennials-gen-x-and-post-millennials. Last accessed January 10, 2019.
2. Center for Disease Control and Prevention. "Suicide Among Youth." Accessed November 15, 2018. https://www.cdc.gov/healthcommunication/toolstemplates/entertainmented/tips/SuicideYouth.html.
3. Ducharme, Jamie. "Drugs, Alchohol and Suicide Are Killing So Many Young Americans That the Country's Average Lifespan Is Falling." *Time Magazine Online*, September 21, 2018. http://time.com/5400566/cdc-mortality-report/. Last accessed November 15, 2018.
4. Petronzio, M. "Millennials Experience Depression at Work More Than Any Other Generation, Study Finds." *Mashable*, May 21, 2015. https://mashable.com/2015/05/21/millennials-depression-work/#EitT.AB_JsqN. Last accessed Nov. 20, 2018.

5. Reiss, Jana. "Why Millennials Are Really Leaving Religion (It's Not Just Politics, Folks)." *Religion News Online: Flunking Sainthood.* June 26, 2018. https://religionnews.com/2018/06/26/why-millennials-are-really-leaving-religion-its-not-just-politics-folks/. Last accessed January 9, 2019.

6. Ratner, Paul. "Religion Isn't Going Anywhere, but the Demographics Are Shifting Dramatically." April 27, 2018. https://bigthink.com/paul-ratner/which-world-religion-will-dominate-in-the-future. Last Accessed January 10, 2019.

7. Samuel, S. "The Witches of Baltimore." *The Atlantic,* November 5, 2018. https://www.theatlantic.com/international/archive/2018/11/black-millennials-african-witchcraft-christianity/574393/. Accessed November 20, 2018.

8. Ratner, Paul. "Religion Isn't Going Anywhere, but the Demographics Are Shifting Dramatically." April 27, 2018. https://bigthink.com/paul-ratner/which-world-religion-will-dominate-in-the-future. Last Accessed January 10, 2019.

9. Galang, Arlyn. "Marketing Struggles Towards the Unreachable Generation." *Medium* Online. November 28, 2017. https://medium.com/@argalang/marketing-struggles-towards-the-unreachable-generation-611709668fd4. Last Accessed January 10, 2019.

10. Moore, Brian. "The Worst Generation?" *The New York Post.* May 10, 2010. https://nypost.com/2010/05/10/the-worst-generation/. Last Accessed January 10, 2019.

11. Center for Disease Control and Prevention. "Suicide Among Youth." Accessed November 15, 2018. https://www.cdc.gov/healthcommunication/toolstemplates/entertainmented/tips/SuicideYouth.html.

12. Center for Disease Control and Prevention. "Suicide Among Youth." Accessed November 15, 2018. https://www.cdc.gov/healthcommunication/toolstemplates/entertainmented/tips/SuicideYouth.html.

13. Ducharme, Jamie. "Drugs, Alchohol and Suicide Are Killing So Many

Young Americans That the Country's Average Lifespan Is Falling." *Time Magazine Online*, September 21, 2018. http://time.com/5400566/cdc-mortality-report/. Last accessed November 15, 2018.

14. Ducharme, Jamie. "Drugs, Alchohol and Suicide Are Killing So Many Young Americans That the Country's Average Lifespan Is Falling." *Time Magazine Online*, September 21, 2018. http://time.com/5400566/cdc-mortality-report/. Last accessed November 15, 2018.

15. Ducharme, Jamie. "Drugs, Alchohol and Suicide Are Killing So Many Young Americans That the Country's Average Lifespan Is Falling." *Time Magazine Online*, September 21, 2018. http://time.com/5400566/cdc-mortality-report/. Last accessed November 15, 2018.

16. Ducharme, Jamie. "Drugs, Alchohol and Suicide Are Killing So Many Young Americans That the Country's Average Lifespan Is Falling." *Time Magazine Online*, September 21, 2018. http://time.com/5400566/cdc-mortality-report/. Last accessed November 15, 2018.

17. Center for Disease Control and Prevention. "Suicide Among Youth." Accessed November 15, 2018. https://www.cdc.gov/healthcommunication/toolstemplates/entertainmented/tips/SuicideYouth.html.

18. Center for Disease Control and Prevention. "Suicide Among Youth." Accessed November 15, 2018. https://www.cdc.gov/healthcommunication/toolstemplates/entertainmented/tips/SuicideYouth.html.

19. Ducharme, Jamie. "Drugs, Alchohol and Suicide Are Killing So Many Young Americans That the Country's Average Lifespan Is Falling." *Time Magazine Online*, September 21, 2018. http://time.com/5400566/cdc-mortality-report/. Last accessed November 15, 2018.

20. "Overdose Death Rates." *National Institute on Drug Abuse*. Accessed November 15, 2018. https://www.drugabuse.gov/related-topics/trends-statistics/overdose-death-rates.

21. Ducharme, Jamie. "Drugs, Alchohol and Suicide Are Killing So Many Young Americans That the Country's Average Lifespan Is Falling." *Time*

Magazine Online, September 21, 2018. http://time.com/5400566/cdc-mortality-report/. Last accessed November 15, 2018.

22. Tapper, E. with Parikh, N. "Alcohol-related Cirrhosis Deaths Skyrocket in Young Adults." *Institute for Healthcare Policy and Innovation for the University of Michigan*. Last Accessed November 15, 2018. http://ihpi.umich.edu/news/alcohol-related-cirrhosis-deaths-skyrocket-young-adults.

23. Tapper, E. with Parikh, N. "Alcohol-related Cirrhosis Deaths Skyrocket in Young Adults." *Institute for Healthcare Policy and Innovation for the University of Michigan*. Last Accessed November 15, 2018. http://ihpi.umich.edu/news/alcohol-related-cirrhosis-deaths-skyrocket-young-adults.

24. Tapper, E. with Parikh, N. "Alcohol-related Cirrhosis Deaths Skyrocket in Young Adults." *Institute for Healthcare Policy and Innovation for the University of Michigan*. Last Accessed November 15, 2018. http://ihpi.umich.edu/news/alcohol-related-cirrhosis-deaths-skyrocket-young-adults.

25. Petronzio, M. "Millennials Experience Depression at Work More Than Any Other eneration, Study Finds." *Mashable*, May 21, 2015. https://mashable.com/2015/05/21/millennials-depression-work/#EitT.AB_JsqN. Last accessed Nov. 20, 2018.

26. Gander, K. "Millennials Are the Most Anxious Generation, New Research Shows." *NewsWeek Online*, May 9, 2018. https://www.newsweek.com/millennials-most-anxious-generation-new-research-shows-917095. Accessed November 20, 2018.

27. Gemino, M. "Millennials: The Most Anxious Generation." *Garden of Life*, August 7, 2018. https://www.gardenoflife.com/content/millennials-anxious-generation/. Accessed November 20, 2018.

28. Wylie, M. "Millennials First in Single-mother Households." *BizJournals*, September 15, 2017. https://www.bizjournals.com/bizwomen/news/latest-news/2017/09/millennials-first-in-single-mother-households.html. Accessed November 20,2018.

29. Wylie, M. "Millennials First in Single-mother Households." *BizJournals*, September 15, 2017. https://www.bizjournals.com/bizwomen/news/

latest-news/2017/09/millennials-first-in-single-mother-households.html. Accessed November 20,2018.

30. http://peacemaker.net/project/the-effects-of-divorce-on-america/

31. Malamut, M. "Witch Population Doubles as Millennials Cast Off Christianity." *New York Times*, November 20, 2018. https://nypost. com/2018/11/20/witch-population-doubles-as-millennials-cast-off-christianity/. Accessed November 20, 2018.

32. Malamut, M. "Witch Population Doubles as Millennials Cast Off Christianity." *New York Times*, November 20, 2018. https://nypost. com/2018/11/20/witch-population-doubles-as-millennials-cast-off-christianity/. Accessed November 20, 2018.

33. Samuel, S. "The Witches of Baltimore." *The Atlantic*, November 5, 2018. https://www.theatlantic.com/international/archive/2018/11/black-millennials-african-witchcraft-christianity/574393/. Accessed November 20, 2018.

34. Samuel, S. "The Witches of Baltimore." *The Atlantic*, November 5, 2018. https://www.theatlantic.com/international/archive/2018/11/black-millennials-african-witchcraft-christianity/574393/. Accessed November 20, 2018.

35. Samuel, S. "The Witches of Baltimore." *The Atlantic*, November 5, 2018. https://www.theatlantic.com/international/archive/2018/11/black-millennials-african-witchcraft-christianity/574393/. Accessed November 20, 2018.

36. Eaton, S. "12 Reasons Millennials Are Over Church." *Recklessly Alive*, September 29, 2016. https://www.recklesslyalive.com/12-reasons-millennials-are-over-church/. Accessed November 20, 2018.

37. Eaton, S. "12 Reasons Millennials Are Over Church." *Recklessly Alive*, September 29, 2016. https://www.recklesslyalive.com/12-reasons-millennials-are-over-church/. Accessed November 20, 2018.

38. Zemeckis, R.obert, dir. *Castaway*. United States: Twentieth Century Fox, Dreamworks, 2000. DVD. 2hours 24 min.

39. Semega, J; Fontenot, MK; Kollar, MA. "What Is the Current Poverty Rate in the United States?" October 15, 2018. https://poverty.ucdavis. edu/faq/what-current-poverty-rate-united-states. Last Accessed January 10, 2019.

40. "Poverty." *UNESCO Online (United Nations Educational, Scientific and Cultural Organization)*. http://www.unesco.org/new/en/social-and-human-sciences/themes/international-migration/glossary/poverty/. Accessed January 10, 2019.

41. "Poverty." *UNESCO Online (United Nations Educational, Scientific and Cultural Organization)*. http://www.unesco.org/new/en/social-and-human-sciences/themes/international-migration/glossary/poverty/. Accessed January 10, 2019.

42. "Generation gap." *Cambridge Dictionary Online*. https://dictionary. cambridge.org/us/dictionary/english/generation-gap. Last Accessed January 10, 2019.

43. Wilkerson, David with Sherrill, John and Elizabeth. 1963. *The Cross and the Switchblade*. USA, published for Teen Challenge by Pyramid Publications by arrangement with Bernard Geis Associates. P. 29.

44. Murray, Don dir. *The Cross and the Switchblade.*United States: Gateway Productions, 1970. DVD, 1 hour, 46 minutes. Timestamp 36:51.

45. Murray, Don dir. *The Cross and the Switchblade.*United States: Gateway Productions, 1970. DVD, 1 hour, 46 minutes.

46. Murray, Don dir. *The Cross and the Switchblade.*United States: Gateway Productions, 1970. DVD, 1 hour, 46 minutes.

47. Murray, Don dir. *The Cross and the Switchblade.*United States: Gateway Productions, 1970. DVD, 1 hour, 46 minutes.

48. Murray, Don dir. *The Cross and the Switchblade.*United States: Gateway Productions, 1970. DVD, 1 hour, 46 minutes. Timestamp 38:12-39:10.

49. Wilkerson, David with Sherrill, John and Elizabeth. 1963. *The Cross and the Switchblade*. USA, published for Teen Challenge by Pyramid Publications by arrangement with Bernard Geis Associates. P. 29.

50. Galang, Arlyn. "Marketing Struggles Towards the Unreachable Generation." *Medium* Online. November 28, 2017. https://medium.com/@argalang/marketing-struggles-towards-the-unreachable-generation-611709668fd4. Last Accessed January 10, 2019.

51. For King and Country. "Epilogue." Recorded 2014. Track 17 bonus on *Run Wild. Live Free. Love Strong.* Fervent Records. Compact Disc.

52. Moore, Brian. "The Worst Generation?" *The New York Post.* May 10, 2010. https://nypost.com/2010/05/10/the-worst-generation/. Last Accessed January 10, 2019.

53. Galang, Arlyn. "Marketing Struggles Towards the Unreachable Generation." *Medium* Online. November 28, 2017. https://medium.com/@argalang/marketing-struggles-towards-the-unreachable-generation-611709668fd4. Last Accessed January 10, 2019.

54. Stein, Joel. "Millennials: The Me Me Me Generation." *Time Magazine Online.* May 20, 2013. http://time.com/247/millennials-the-me-me-me-generation/. Last accessed January 15, 2019.

55. Gander, Kashmira. "Millennials Are the Most Anxious Generation, New Research Shows." *Newsweek Online.* May 8, 2018. https://www.newsweek.com/millennials-most-anxious-generation-new-research-shows-917095. Last accessed January 10, 2019.

56. Perry, Philip. "Millennials Are at Higher Risk for Mental Health Issues. This May Be Why. " *The Big Think.* January 8, 2018. https://bigthink.com/philip-perry/millennials-are-at-higher-risk-for-mental-health-issues-this-may-be-why. Last Accessed January 10, 2019.

57. Dixon, Emily. "Why Do I Feel So Lonely? Millennials Are Unhappier Than Previous Generations, According to New Research." August 10, 2018. https://www.bustle.com/p/why-do-i-feel-so-lonely-millennials-are-unhappier-than-previous-generations-according-to-new-research-10051122. Last Accessed January 10, 2019.

58. Stevens, Heidi. "Young Americans Are the Loneliest Generation, and Their Phones Aren't to Blame." *The Chicago Tribune.* May 3, 2018.

https://www.chicagotribune.com/lifestyles/stevens/ct-life-stevens-thursday-americans-are-lonely-0503-story.html. Last accessed January 10, 2019.

59. Tiwana, Simrit. "Here's Why Millennials Are Considered the Most Lonely Generation of All Time." *Cosmopolitan.* September 4, 2018. https://www.cosmopolitan.in/life/features/a15768/heres-why-millennials-are-considered-most-lonely-generation-all-time. Last accessed January 10, 2019.

60. Dorrough, Jeremy. "The Fatherless Generation." *Prezi Online.* September 11, 2013. https://prezi.com/yocg67qhinhj/the-fatherless-generation/. Last accessed January 10, 2019.

61. Wesley, John. "John Wesley>Quotes>Quotable Quote." Goodreads. https://www.goodreads.com/quotes/349175-what-one-generation-tolerates-the-next-generation-will-embrace. Accessed December 5, 2018.

62. Groothuis, Douglas. *Truth Decay: Defending Christianity Against the Challenges of PostmodernismI.* Downers Grove, IL: Green Press, 2000, p. 33.

63. "History.com Editors." *History.com.* Accessed December 5, 2018. https://www.history.com/topics/renaissance/renaissance.

64. "History.com Editors." *History.com.* Accessed December 5, 2018. https://www.history.com/topics/renaissance/renaissance.

65. Groothuis, Douglas. *Truth Decay: Defending Christianity Against the Challenges of PostmodernismI.* Downers Grove, IL: Green Press, 2000, p. 34.

66. Groothuis, Douglas. *Truth Decay: Defending Christianity Against the Challenges of PostmodernismI.* Downers Grove, IL: Green Press, 2000, p. 34.

67. "History.com Editors." *History.com.* Accessed December 5, 2018. https://www.history.com/topics/renaissance/renaissance.

68. Groothuis, Douglas. *Truth Decay: Defending Christianity Against the Challenges of PostmodernismI.* Downers Grove, IL: Green Press, 2000, p. 35.

69. Groothuis, Douglas. *Truth Decay: Defending Christianity Against the Challenges of PostmodernismI.* Downers Grove, IL: Green Press, 2000, p. 37.

70. Friedrich Nietzche, "The Gay Science," 125, in *The Portable Nietzsche*, trans. Walter Kaufmann (New York: Viking, 1968), p. 95.

71. Groothuis, Douglas. *Truth Decay: Defending Christianity Against the Challenges of PostmodernismI.* Downers Grove, IL: Green Press, 2000, p. 38.

72. Groothuis, Douglas. *Truth Decay: Defending Christianity Against the Challenges of PostmodernismI.* Downers Grove, IL: Green Press, 2000, p. 39-40.

73. Groothuis, Douglas. *Truth Decay: Defending Christianity Against the Challenges of PostmodernismI.* Downers Grove, IL: Green Press, 2000, p. 39-40.

74. Groothuis, Douglas. *Truth Decay: Defending Christianity Against the Challenges of PostmodernismI.* Downers Grove, IL: Green Press, 2000, p. 40.

75. *Merriam-Webster Dictionary: Secularism.* (2018) Accessed December 11 2018. https://www.merriam-webster.com/dictionary/secularism.

76. The Veritas Forum. "Is Tolerance Intolerant? Pursuing the Climate of Acceptance and Inclusion." February 17, 2013. YouTube Video, 1:46:43. https://www.youtube.com/watch?v=uyTa5r4GG4M. Accessed December 11, 2018.

77. The Veritas Forum. "Is Tolerance Intolerant? Pursuing the Climate of Acceptance and Inclusion." February 17, 2013. YouTube Video, 1:46:43. https://www.youtube.com/watch?v=uyTa5r4GG4M. Accessed December 11, 2018.

78. *Merriam-Webster Dictionary: Pluralism.* (2018) Accessed December 11 2018. https://www.merriam-webster.com/dictionary/pluralism.

79. The Veritas Forum. "Is Tolerance Intolerant? Pursuing the Climate of Acceptance and Inclusion." February 17, 2013. YouTube Video, 1:46:43. https://www.youtube.com/watch?v=uyTa5r4GG4M. Accessed December 11, 2018.

80. *Merriam-Webster Dictionary: Privatize.* (2018) Accessed December 11 2018. https://www.merriam-webster.com/dictionary/privatize.

81. The Veritas Forum. "Is Tolerance Intolerant? Pursuing the Climate

of Acceptance and Inclusion." February 17, 2013. YouTube Video, 1:46:43. https://www.youtube.com/watch?v=uyTa5r4GG4M. Accessed December 11, 2018.

82. Schmall, Tyler. "Millennials Don't Know Their Neighbors at All." *The New York Post.* July 10, 2018. https://nypost.com/2018/07/10/millennials-are-horrible-neighbors/. Last accessed January 10, 2019.

83. Schmall, Tyler. "Millennials Don't Know Their Neighbors at All." *The New York Post.* July 10, 2018. https://nypost.com/2018/07/10/millennials-are-horrible-neighbors/. Last accessed January 10, 2019.

84. Schmall, Tyler. "Millennials Don't Know Their Neighbors at All." *The New York Post.* July 10, 2018. https://nypost.com/2018/07/10/millennials-are-horrible-neighbors/. Last accessed January 10, 2019.

85. Le Penne, Shirley. "Longing to Belong: Needing to Be Needed in a World in Need." Society, Volume 54, Issue 6, pp. 535–536. December 2017. https://link.springer.com/article/10.1007/s12115-017-0185-y. Last accessed January 10, 2019.

86. Le Penne, Shirley. "Longing to Belong: Needing to Be Needed in a World in Need." Society, Volume 54, Issue 6, pp. 535–536. December 2017. https://link.springer.com/article/10.1007/s12115-017-0185-y. Last accessed January 10, 2019.

87. Le Penne, Shirley. "Longing to Belong: Needing to be Needed in a World in Need." Society, Volume 54, Issue 6, pp. 535–536. December 2017. https://link.springer.com/article/10.1007/s12115-017-0185-y. Last accessed January 10, 2019.

88. Osborne, Evan. "The Diversity Ideology." *The Quillette.* February 12, 2018. https://quillette.com/2018/02/12/the-diversity-ideology/. Last accessed January 11, 2019.

89. Osborne, Evan. "The Diversity Ideology." *The Quillette.* February 12, 2018. https://quillette.com/2018/02/12/the-diversity-ideology/. Last accessed January 11, 2019.

90. Let Freedom Speak: The Daily Signal. "How 'Diversity Delusion' infiltrated College Campuses." 2018. https://www.facebook.com/

LetFreedomSpeak/videos/349262402312686/. Last accessed January 11, 2019.

91. Feldmann, Derrick. "Millennials Are Engaging in Political Action Now More Than Ever." October 11, 2017. https://impact.vice.com/en_us/article/gy57km/millennials-are-engaging-in-political-action-now-more-than-ever. Last accessed January 10, 2019.

92. Burstein, David. "Are Millennials Better Activists Than Baby Boomers?" *Mic Network*. March 26, 2013. https://mic.com/articles/30658/are-millennials-better-activists-than-baby-boomers#.zR2861TLK. Last accessed January 10, 2019.

93. Burstein, David. "Are Millennials Better Activists Than Baby Boomers?" *Mic Network*. March 26, 2013. https://mic.com/articles/30658/are-millennials-better-activists-than-baby-boomers#.zR2861TLK. Last accessed January 10, 2019.

94. Gronlund, Jay. "How Newly-Energized Millennial Activists Are Shaping Brand Choices." *Business 2 Community Online*. March 22, 2018. https://www.business2community.com/branding/newly-energized-millennial-activists-shaping-brand-choices-02031863. Last accessed January 10, 2019.

95. "Isolate." *Merriam-Webster Online*. https://www.merriam-webster.com/dictionary/isolate. Last accessed January 11, 2019.

96. TedX Talks: TEDxVermilion Street. "What Teenagers Want You to Know: Roy Petitfils." October 11, 2016. 17:55. https://www.youtube.com/watch?v=fC2z69q3L0o. Last accessed January 11, 2019.

97. TedX Talks: TEDxVermilion Street. "What Teenagers Want You to Know: Roy Petitfils." October 11, 2016. 17:55. https://www.youtube.com/watch?v=fC2z69q3L0o. Last accessed January 11, 2019.

98. TedX Talks: TEDxVermilion Street. "What Teenagers Want You to Know: Roy Petitfils." October 11, 2016. 17:55. https://www.youtube.com/watch?v=fC2z69q3L0o. Last accessed January 11, 2019.

99. TedX Talks: TEDxVermilion Street. "What Teenagers Want You to Know: Roy Petitfils." October 11, 2016. 17:55. https://www.youtube.com/watch?v=fC2z69q3L0o. Last accessed January 11, 2019.

100. TedX Talks: TEDxToronto. "Why we choose suicide: Mark Henick." October 1, 2013. YouTube Video, 15:25. https://www.youtube.com/watch?v=D1QoyTmeAYw. Last accessed January 11, 2019.

101. TedX Talks: TEDxToronto. "Why we choose suicide: Mark Henick." October 1, 2013. YouTube Video, 15:25. https://www.youtube.com/watch?v=D1QoyTmeAYw. Last accessed January 11, 2019.

102. TedX Talks: TEDxToronto. "Why We Choose Suicide: Mark Henick." October 1, 2013. YouTube Video, 15:25. https://www.youtube.com/watch?v=D1QoyTmeAYw. Last accessed January 11, 2019.

103. *Merriam-Webster Dictionary Online*, (2018), "Identity." https://www.merriam-webster.com/dictionary/identity. Accessed December 18, 2018.

104. The Audopedia. "What Is Identity Politics? What does Identity Politics mean? Identity Politics Meaning." December 12, 2016. YouTube Video, 6:10. https://www.youtube.com/watch?v=6Feru5rVoMQ. Accessed December 12, 2018.

105. "What Does Your Last Name Say About You?" *Ancestry.com.* Accessed December 12, 2018. https://blogs.ancestry.com/cm/there-are-7-types-of-english-surnames-which-one-is-yours/.

106. "What Does Your Last Name Say About You?" *Ancestry.com.* Accessed December 12, 2018. https://blogs.ancestry.com/cm/there-are-7-types-of-english-surnames-which-one-is-yours/.

107. "What Does Your Last Name Say About You?" *Ancestry.com.* Accessed December 12, 2018. https://blogs.ancestry.com/cm/there-are-7-types-of-english-surnames-which-one-is-yours/.

108. Berk, L. (2018). Development Through the Lifespan. Hoboken, NJ: Pearson Education, Inc. pp. 258.

109. Berk, L. (2018). Development Through the Lifespan. Hoboken, NJ: Pearson Education, Inc. pp. 258.

110. Berk, L. (2018). Development Through the Lifespan. Hoboken, NJ: Pearson Education, Inc. pp. 260.

111. Berk, L. (2018). Development Through the Lifespan. Hoboken, NJ: Pearson Education, Inc. pp. 336.

112. Berk, L. (2018). Development Through the Lifespan. Hoboken, NJ: Pearson Education, Inc. pp. 336.

113. Berk, L. (2018). Development Through the Lifespan. Hoboken, NJ: Pearson Education, Inc. pp. 337.

114. Berk, L. (2018). Development Through the Lifespan. Hoboken, NJ: Pearson Education, Inc. pp. 339.

115. Berk, L. (2018). Development Through the Lifespan. Hoboken, NJ: Pearson Education, Inc. pp. 408.

116. Berk, L. (2018). Development Through the Lifespan. Hoboken, NJ: Pearson Education, Inc. pp. 408.

117. Berk, L. (2018). Development Through the Lifespan. Hoboken, NJ: Pearson Education, Inc. pp. 408.

118. Berk, L. (2018). Development Through the Lifespan. Hoboken, NJ: Pearson Education, Inc. pp. 408.

119. Berk, L. (2018). Development Through the Lifespan. Hoboken, NJ: Pearson Education, Inc. pp. 538.

120. Berk, L. (2018). Development Through the Lifespan. Hoboken, NJ: Pearson Education, Inc. pp.610.

121. Berk, L. (2018). Development Through the Lifespan. Hoboken, NJ: Pearson Education, Inc. pp. 539.

122. Berk, L. (2018). Development Through the Lifespan. Hoboken, NJ: Pearson Education, Inc. pp. 539.

123. Berk, L. (2018). Development Through the Lifespan. Hoboken, NJ: Pearson Education, Inc. pp. 537.

124. Moore, Brian. "The Worst Generation?" *The New York Post.* May 10, 2018. https://nypost.com/2010/05/10/the-worst-generation/. Accessed December 18, 2019.

125. Burke, Daniel. "Millennials Leaving Church in Droves, Study Finds," *CNN Online*, May 14, 2015. https://www.cnn.com/2015/05/12/living/pew-religion-study/index.html. Accessed December 18, 2018.

126. Berk, L. (2018). Development Through the Lifespan. Hoboken, NJ: Pearson Education, Inc. pp. 541.

127. The Veritas Forum. "Is Tolerance Intolerant? Pursuing the Climate of Acceptance and Inclusion." February 17, 2013. YouTube Video, 1:46:43. https://www.youtube.com/watch?v=uyTa5r4GG4M. Accessed December 11, 2018.

128. The Veritas Forum. "Is Tolerance Intolerant? Pursuing the Climate of Acceptance and Inclusion." February 17, 2013. YouTube Video, 1:46:43. https://www.youtube.com/watch?v=uyTa5r4GG4M. Accessed December 11, 2018.

129. Berk, L. (2018). Development Through the Lifespan. Hoboken, NJ: Pearson Education, Inc. pp. 523.

130. The Veritas Forum. "Is Tolerance Intolerant? Pursuing the Climate of Acceptance and Inclusion." February 17, 2013. YouTube Video, 1:46:43. https://www.youtube.com/watch?v=uyTa5r4GG4M. Accessed December 11, 2018.

131. The Veritas Forum. "Is Tolerance Intolerant? Pursuing the Climate of Acceptance and Inclusion." February 17, 2013. YouTube Video, 1:46:43. https://www.youtube.com/watch?v=uyTa5r4GG4M. Accessed December 11, 2018.

132. The Veritas Forum. "Is Tolerance Intolerant? Pursuing the Climate of Acceptance and Inclusion." February 17, 2013. YouTube Video, 1:46:43. https://www.youtube.com/watch?v=uyTa5r4GG4M. Accessed December 11, 2018.

133. Tedx Talks St. Louis Women. "It's About Time We Stop Shaming Millennials. Lindsey Pollak." Nov. 15, 2016. YouTube Video, 13:55. https://www.youtube.com/watch?v=kaCQ-giZOxg. Accessed Oct. 30, 2018.

134. Tedx Talks St. Louis Women. "It's About Time We Stop Shaming Millennials. Lindsey Pollak." Nov. 15, 2016. YouTube Video, 13:55. https://www.youtube.com/watch?v=kaCQ-giZOxg. Accessed Oct. 30, 2018.

135. Tedx Talks St. Louis Women. "It's About Time We Stop Shaming Millennials. Lindsey Pollak." Nov. 15, 2016. YouTube Video, 13:55.

https://www.youtube.com/watch?v=kaCQ-giZOxg. Accessed Oct. 30, 2018.

136. "Child Care: Trends in child care." *Child Trends*. Accessed January , 2019. https://www.childtrends.org/indicators/child-care.

137. Sondheim, S. (2011). Children Will Listen. On *Into the Woods*. [CD]. New York, NY: Masterworks.

138. Waters, T. E. A., Raby, K. L., Ruiz, S. K., Martin, J., & Roisman, G. I. "Adult Attachment Representations and the Quality of Romantic and Parent-child Relationships: An Examination of the Contributions of Coherence of Discourse and Secure Base Script Knowledge." *Developmental Psychology: Advance online publication.* 2018. http://0-dx. doi.org.library.regent.edu/10.1037/dev0000607. Accessed Oct. 30, 2018.

139. Berk, Laura. *Development Through the Lifespan*. Hoboken: New Jersey: Pearson Education, 2018. pp.236.

140. "Television and Children." *University of Michigan: Michigan Medicine.* Accessed January 4, 2019. http://www.med.umich.edu/yourchild/topics/tv.

141. "Television and Children." *University of Michigan: Michigan Medicine.* Accessed January 4, 2019. http://www.med.umich.edu/yourchild/topics/tv.

142. "Television and Children." *University of Michigan: Michigan Medicine.* Accessed January 4, 2019. http://www.med.umich.edu/yourchild/topics/tv.

143. "Television and Children." *University of Michigan: Michigan Medicine.* Accessed January 4, 2019. http://www.med.umich.edu/yourchild/topics/tv.

144. "Television and Children." *University of Michigan: Michigan Medicine.* Accessed January 4, 2019. http://www.med.umich.edu/yourchild/topics/tv.

145. Berk, Laura. *Development Through the Lifespan*.Hoboken: New Jersey: Pearson Education, 2018. pp.157.

146. "Television and Children." *University of Michigan: Michigan Medicine.* Accessed January 4, 2019. http://www.med.umich.edu/yourchild/topics/tv.

147. Berk, Laura. *Development Through the Lifespan.*Hoboken: New Jersey: Pearson Education, 2018. pp.217.

148. Berk, Laura. *Development Through the Lifespan.*Hoboken: New Jersey: Pearson Education, 2018. pp.217.

149. Dunckley, Victoria. "Gray Matters: Too Much Screen Time Damages the Brain." *Psychology Today.* February 27, 2019. https://www.psychologytoday.com/us/blog/mental-wealth/201402/gray-matters-too-much-screen-time-damages-the-brain. Last accessed January 4, 2019.

150. Brophy, Kate. "What Is Dopamine? Understanding the "Feel-Good Hormone." *University Health News Daily.* October 18, 2018. https://universityhealthnews.com/daily/depression/what-is-dopamine-understanding-the-feel-good-hormone/. Last accessed March 6, 2019.

151. Dunckley, Victoria. "Gray Matters: Too Much Screen Time Damages the Brain." *Psychology Today.* February 27, 2019. https://www.psychologytoday.com/us/blog/mental-wealth/201402/gray-matters-too-much-screen-time-damages-the-brain. Last accessed January 4, 2019.

152. Dunckley, Victoria. "Gray Matters: Too Much Screen Time Damages the Brain." *Psychology Today.* February 27, 2019. https://www.psychologytoday.com/us/blog/mental-wealth/201402/gray-matters-too-much-screen-time-damages-the-brain. Last accessed January 4, 2019.

153. Berk, Laura. *Development Through the Lifespan.*Hoboken: New Jersey: Pearson Education, 2018. pp.124.

154. Berk, Laura. *Development Through the Lifespan.*Hoboken: New Jersey: Pearson Education, 2018. pp.124.

155. Kamenetz, Anya. "Screen Addiciton Among Teens: Is There Such a

Thing?" *National Public Radio Online*. February 5, 2018. https://www. npr.org/sections/ed/2018/02/05/579554273/screen-addiction-among-teens-is-there-such-a-thing. Last Accessed January 4, 2019.

156. Graham, Judith and Forstadt, Leslie. "How Television Viewing Affects Children." *Extension: University of Maine*. 2011. https://extension. umaine.edu/publications/4100e/. Last Accessed January 4, 2019.

157. Graham, Judith and Forstadt, Leslie. "How Television Viewing Affects Children." *Extension: University of Maine*. 2011. https://extension. umaine.edu/publications/4100e/. Last Accessed January 4, 2019.

158. Graham, Judith and Forstadt, Leslie. "How Television Viewing Affects Children." *Extension: University of Maine*. 2011. https://extension. umaine.edu/publications/4100e/. Last Accessed January 4, 2019.

159. Graham, Judith and Forstadt, Leslie. "How Television Viewing Affects Children." *Extension: University of Maine*. 2011. https://extension. umaine.edu/publications/4100e/. Last Accessed January 4, 2019.

160. Beaton, Caroline. "Why Millennials Are Lonely." *Forbes Online*. February 9, 2019. https://www.forbes.com/ sites/carolinebeaton/2017/02/09/why-millennials-are-lonely/#2e60aa647c35. Last accessed January 4, 2019.

161. Perry, Philip. "Millennials Are at Higher Risk for Mental Health Issues. This May Be Why." *The Big Think*. January 8, 2018. https://bigthink. com/philip-perry/millennials-are-at-higher-risk-for-mental-health-issues-this-may-be-why. Last accessed January 11, 2019.

162. Perry, Philip. "Millennials Are at Higher Risk for Mental Health Issues. This May Be Why." *The Big Think*. January 8, 2018. https://bigthink. com/philip-perry/millennials-are-at-higher-risk-for-mental-health-issues-this-may-be-why. Last accessed January 11, 2019.

163. Perry, Philip. "Millennials Are at Higher Risk for Mental Health Issues. This May Be Why." *The Big Think*. January 8, 2018. https://bigthink. com/philip-perry/millennials-are-at-higher-risk-for-mental-health-issues-this-may-be-why. Last accessed January 11, 2019.

164. Perry, Philip. "Millennials Are at Higher Risk for Mental Health Issues.

This May Be Why." *The Big Think.* January 8, 2018. https://bigthink. com/philip-perry/millennials-are-at-higher-risk-for-mental-health-issues-this-may-be-why. Last accessed January 11, 2019.

165. Perry, Philip. "Millennials Are at Higher Risk for Mental Health Issues. This May Be Why." *The Big Think.* January 8, 2018. https://bigthink. com/philip-perry/millennials-are-at-higher-risk-for-mental-health-issues-this-may-be-why. Last accessed January 11, 2019.

166. Clark, Bob, dir. *A Christmas Story.* United States: Warner Brothers, 1983. DVD. 94 min.

167. Clark, Bob, dir. *A Christmas Story.* United States: Warner Brothers, 1983. DVD. 94 min.

168. Clark, Bob, dir. *A Christmas Story.* United States: Warner Brothers, 1983. DVD. 94 min.

169. Johnson, Caitlin. "Cutting Through Advertising Clutter." *CBS News.* September 17, 2006. https://www.cbsnews.com/news/cutting-through-advertising-clutter/. Last accessed January 3, 2019.

170. Smith, Noah. "The 2000s Sure Were a Horrible Decade for the U.S." *Bloomberg News, Newsday Online.* January 29, 2015. https://www. newsday.com/opinion/oped/the-2000s-sure-were-a-horrible-decade-for-the-u-s-noah-smith-1.9876065. Last accessed January 4, 2019.

171. Smith, Noah. "The 2000s Sure Were a Horrible Decade for the U.S." *Bloomberg News, Newsday Online.* January 29, 2015. https://www. newsday.com/opinion/oped/the-2000s-sure-were-a-horrible-decade-for-the-u-s-noah-smith-1.9876065. Last accessed January 4, 2019.

172. Smith, Noah. "The 2000s Sure Were a Horrible Decade for the U.S." *Bloomberg News, Newsday Online.* January 29, 2015. https://www. newsday.com/opinion/oped/the-2000s-sure-were-a-horrible-decade-for-the-u-s-noah-smith-1.9876065. Last accessed January 4, 2019.

173. Kurt, Daniel. "How the Financial Crisis Affected Millennials." *Investopedia Insights: Markets & Economy.* September 13, 2018. https://www.investopedia.com/insights/how-financial-crisis-affected-millennials/. Last Accessed January 4, 2019.

174. Smith, Noah. "The 2000s Sure Were a Horrible Decade for the U.S." *Bloomberg News, Newsday Online.* January 29, 2015. https://www.newsday.com/opinion/oped/the-2000s-sure-were-a-horrible-decade-for-the-u-s-noah-smith-1.9876065. Last accessed January 4, 2019.

175. Foley, Meghan. "This Is What the Recession Did to Millennials." *The Cheat Sheet.* May 13, 2015. https://www.cheatsheet.com/politics/this-is-what-the-recession-did-to-millennials.html/. Last Accessed January 3, 2019.

176. Kurt, Daniel. "How the Financial Crisis Affected Millennials." *Investopedia Insights: Markets & Economy.* September 13, 2018. https://www.investopedia.com/insights/how-financial-crisis-affected-millennials/. Last Accessed January 4, 2019.

177. Foley, Meghan. "This Is What the Recession Did to Millennials." *The Cheat Sheet.* May 13, 2015. https://www.cheatsheet.com/politics/this-is-what-the-recession-did-to-millennials.html/. Last Accessed January 3, 2019.

178. Foley, Meghan. "This Is What the Recession Did to Millennials." *The Cheat Sheet.* May 13, 2015. https://www.cheatsheet.com/politics/this-is-what-the-recession-did-to-millennials.html/. Last Accessed January 3, 2019.

179. Foley, Meghan. "This Is What the Recession Did to Millennials." *The Cheat Sheet.* May 13, 2015. https://www.cheatsheet.com/politics/this-is-what-the-recession-did-to-millennials.html/. Last Accessed January 3, 2019.

180. Foley, Meghan. "This Is What the Recession Did to Millennials." *The Cheat Sheet.* May 13, 2015. https://www.cheatsheet.com/politics/this-is-what-the-recession-did-to-millennials.html/. Last Accessed January 3, 2019.

181. Foley, Meghan. "This Is What the Recession Did to Millennials." *The Cheat Sheet.* May 13, 2015. https://www.cheatsheet.com/politics/this-is-what-the-recession-did-to-millennials.html/. Last Accessed January 3, 2019.

182. Kurt, Daniel. "How the Financial Crisis Affected Millennials." *Investopedia Insights: Markets & Economy.* September 13, 2018. https://www.investopedia.com/insights/how-financial-crisis-affected-millennials/. Last Accessed January 4, 2019.

183. Kurt, Daniel. "How the Financial Crisis Affected Millennials." *Investopedia Insights: Markets & Economy.* September 13, 2018. https://www.investopedia.com/insights/how-financial-crisis-affected-millennials/. Last Accessed January 4, 2019.

184. Kurt, Daniel. "How the Financial Crisis Affected Millennials." *Investopedia Insights: Markets & Economy.* September 13, 2018. https://www.investopedia.com/insights/how-financial-crisis-affected-millennials/. Last Accessed January 4, 2019.

185. Nova, Annie. "Despite the Economic Recovery, Student Debtors' 'Monster in the Closet' Has Only Worsened." *CNBC.* September 22, 2018. https://www.cnbc.com/2018/09/21/the-student-loan-bubble.html. Last accessed January 2, 2019.

186. Nova, Annie. "Despite the Economic Recovery, Student Debtors' 'Monster in the Closet' Has Only Worsened." *CNBC.* September 22, 2018. https://www.cnbc.com/2018/09/21/the-student-loan-bubble.html. Last accessed January 2, 2019.

187. Capra, Frank, dir. *You Can't Take It With You.* United States: Columbia Pictures Corporation, 1938. DVD. 126 min.

188. Nova, Annie. "Despite the Economic Recovery, Student Debtors' 'Monster in the Closet' Has Only Worsened." *CNBC.* September 22, 2018. https://www.cnbc.com/2018/09/21/the-student-loan-bubble.html. Last accessed January 2, 2019.

189. Nova, Annie. "Despite the Economic Recovery, Student Debtors' 'Monster in the Closet' Has Only Worsened." *CNBC.* September 22, 2018. https://www.cnbc.com/2018/09/21/the-student-loan-bubble.html. Last accessed January 2, 2019.

190. Moore, Brian. "The Worst Generation?" *The New York Post.* May 10,

2010. https://nypost.com/2010/05/10/the-worst-generation/. Last Accessed January 10, 2019.

191. Nova, Annie. "Despite the Economic Recovery, Student Debtors' 'Monster in the Closet' Has Only Worsened." *CNBC.* September 22, 2018. https://www.cnbc.com/2018/09/21/the-student-loan-bubble. html. Last accessed January 2, 2019.

192. Nova, Annie. "Despite the Economic Recovery, Student Debtors' 'Monster in the Closet' Has Only Worsened." *CNBC.* September 22, 2018. https://www.cnbc.com/2018/09/21/the-student-loan-bubble. html. Last accessed January 2, 2019.

193. Nova, Annie. "Despite the Economic Recovery, Student Debtors' 'Monster in the Closet' Has Only Worsened." *CNBC.* September 22, 2018. https://www.cnbc.com/2018/09/21/the-student-loan-bubble. html. Last accessed January 2, 2019.

194. Nova, Annie. "Despite the Economic Recovery, Student Debtors' 'Monster in the Closet' Has Only Worsened." *CNBC.* September 22, 2018. https://www.cnbc.com/2018/09/21/the-student-loan-bubble. html. Last accessed January 2, 2019.

195. Nova, Annie. "Despite the Economic Recovery, Student Debtors' 'Monster in the Closet' Has Only Worsened." *CNBC.* September 22, 2018. https://www.cnbc.com/2018/09/21/the-student-loan-bubble. html. Last accessed January 2, 2019.

196. Sun, Leo: The Motley Fool. "A Foolish Take: Millennials Are Fore Frugal Than You Think." *USA Today Online.* November 4, 2017. https://www.usatoday.com/story/money/personalfinance/2017/11/04/ a-foolish-take-millennials-are-more-frugal-than-you- think/107167056/. Last accessed January 12, 2019.

197. Sun, Leo: The Motley Fool. "A Foolish Take: Millennials Are More Frugal Than You Think." *USA Today Online.* November 4, 2017. https://www.usatoday.com/story/money/personalfinance/2017/11/04/ a-foolish-take-millennials-are-more-frugal-than-you- think/107167056/. Last accessed January 12, 2019.

198. Sun, Leo: The Motley Fool. "A Foolish Take: Millennials Are More Frugal Than You Think." *USA Today Online*. November 4, 2017. https://www.usatoday.com/story/money/personalfinance/2017/11/04/a-foolish-take-millennials-are-more-frugal-than-you-think/107167056/. Last accessed January 12, 2019.

199. Estrada, Donna. "5 Reasons Why Millennials Are a Lot More Thrifty Than Older Generations Think." *Literally Darling*. October 18, 2017. http://www.literallydarling.com/blog/2017/10/18/5-reasons-millennials-lot-thrifty-older-generation-think/. Last accessed January 12, 2019.

200. Estrada, Donna. "5 Reasons Why Millennials Are a Lot More Thrifty Than Older Generations Think." *Literally Darling*. October 18, 2017. http://www.literallydarling.com/blog/2017/10/18/5-reasons-millennials-lot-thrifty-older-generation-think/. Last accessed January 12, 2019.

201. Tedx Talks Salem. "Millennials—Why Are They the Worst? Kelly Williams Brown." Jan. 31, 2014. YouTube Video, 12:18. https://www.youtube.com/watch?v=ygBfwgnijlk. Accessed Oct. 30, 2018.

202. Tedx Talks Salem. "Millennials—Why Are They the worst? Kelly Williams Brown." Jan. 31, 2014. YouTube Video, 12:18. https://www.youtube.com/watch?v=ygBfwgnijlk. Accessed Oct. 30, 2018.

203. Tedx Talks Salem. "Millennials—Why Are They the Worst? Kelly Williams Brown." Jan. 31, 2014. YouTube Video, 12:18. https://www.youtube.com/watch?v=ygBfwgnijlk. Accessed Oct. 30, 2018.

204. Tedx Talks Salem. "Millennials—Why Are They the Worst? Kelly Williams Brown." Jan. 31, 2014. YouTube Video, 12:18. https://www.youtube.com/watch?v=ygBfwgnijlk. Accessed Oct. 30, 2018.

205. Tedx Talks Salem. "Millennials—Why Are They the Worst? Kelly Williams Brown." Jan. 31, 2014. YouTube Video, 12:18. https://www.youtube.com/watch?v=ygBfwgnijlk. Accessed Oct. 30, 2018.

206. Rainier, Thom S. *Becoming a Welcoming Church*. Nashville, Tennessee, B&H Publishing Group, 2017. Pp. 63–64..

207. Earls, Aaron. "7 Ways to Draw Millennials To Your Church." *Facts & Trends Online.* May 20, 2014. https://factsandtrends. net/2014/05/20/7-ways-to-draw-millennials-to-your-church/. Last accessed January 9, 2019.

208. Rainier, Thom S. *Becoming a Welcoming Church.* Nashville, Tennessee, B&H Publishing Group, 2017. Pp. 43.

209. Rainier, Thom S. *Becoming a Welcoming Church.* Nashville, Tennessee, B&H Publishing Group, 2017. Pp. 61.

210. Rainier, Thom S. *Becoming a Welcoming Church.* Nashville, Tennessee, B&H Publishing Group, 2017. Pp. 62.

211. Rainier, Thom S. *Becoming a Welcoming Church.* Nashville, Tennessee, B&H Publishing Group, 2017. Pp. 9.

212. Powell, Frank. "10 Reasons Churches Are Not Reaching Millennials." *Frank Powell Online.* June 25, 2014. http://frankpowell.me/ten-reasons-church-absent-millennials/. Last Accessed January 9, 2019.

213. Evans, Rachel H. "Want Millennials Back in the Pews? Stop Trying to Make Church 'Cool.'" *The Washington Post.* April 30, 2015. https://www.washingtonpost.com/opinions/jesus-doesnt-tweet/2015/04/30/fb07ef1a-ed01-11e4-8666-a1d756d0218e_story. html?noredirect=on&utm_term=.97a37493950d. Last accessed January 9, 2019.

214. Evans, Rachel H. "Want Millennials Back in the Pews? Stop Trying to Make Church 'Cool.'" *The Washington Post.* April 30, 2015. https://www.washingtonpost.com/opinions/jesus-doesnt-tweet/2015/04/30/fb07ef1a-ed01-11e4-8666-a1d756d0218e_story. html?noredirect=on&utm_term=.97a37493950d. Last accessed January 9, 2019.

215. Powell, Frank. "10 Reasons Churches Are Not Reaching Millennials." *Frank Powell Online.* June 25, 2014. http://frankpowell.me/ten-reasons-church-absent-millennials/. Last Accessed January 9, 2019.

216. Wisnewski, Jesse. "Why Many Church Leaders Fail to Reach Millennials (and 5 Things You Can Do About It)." *Catalyst Leader*

Online. April 10, 2018. https://catalystleader.com/read/why-many-church-leaders-fail-to-reach-millennials-and-5-things-you-can-do-a. Last accessed January 9, 2019.

217. Wisnewski, Jesse. "Why Many Church Leaders Fail to Reach Millennials (and 5 Things You Can Do About It)." *Catalyst Leader Online*. April 10, 2018. https://catalystleader.com/read/why-many-church-leaders-fail-to-reach-millennials-and-5-things-you-can-do-a. Last accessed January 9, 2019.

218. Powell, Frank. "10 Reasons Churches Are Not Reaching Millennials." *Frank Powell Online*. June 25, 2014. http://frankpowell.me/ten-reasons-church-absent-millennials/. Last Accessed January 9, 2019.

219. Wisnewski, Jesse. "Why Many Church Leaders Fail to Reach Millennials (and 5 Things You Can Do About It)." *Catalyst Leader Online*. April 10, 2018. https://catalystleader.com/read/why-many-church-leaders-fail-to-reach-millennials-and-5-things-you-can-do-a. Last accessed January 9, 2019.

220. "You Can Lead a Horse to Water…" *BBC Learning English*. http://www.bbc.co.uk/worldservice/learningenglish/language/2012/09/120924_todays_phrase_horse_to_water.sshtm. Last accessed January 14, 2019.

221. Eaton, S. "12 Reasons Millennials Are Over Church." *Recklessly Alive*. September 29, 2016. http://www.recklesslyalive.com/12-reasons-millennials-are-over-church/. Last accessed January 8, 2019.

222. Powell, Frank. "10 Reasons Churches Are Not Reaching Millennials." *Frank Powell Online*. June 25, 2014. http://frankpowell.me/ten-reasons-church-absent-millennials/. Last Accessed January 9, 2019.

223. Powell, Frank. "10 Reasons Churches Are Not Reaching Millennials." *Frank Powell Online*. June 25, 2014. http://frankpowell.me/ten-reasons-church-absent-millennials/. Last Accessed January 9, 2019.

224. Powell, Frank. "10 Reasons Churches Are Not Reaching Millennials." *Frank Powell Online*. June 25, 2014. http://frankpowell.me/ten-reasons-church-absent-millennials/. Last Accessed January 9, 2019.

225. Wisnewski, Jesse. "Why Many Church Leaders Fail to Reach Millennials (and 5 Things You Can Do About It)." *Catalyst Leader Online*. April 10, 2018. https://catalystleader.com/read/why-many-church-leaders-fail-to-reach-millennials-and-5-things-you-can-do-a. Last accessed January 9, 2019.

226. Evans, Rachel H. "Want Millennials Back in the Pews? Stop Trying to Make Church 'Cool.'" *The Washington Post*. April 30, 2015. https://www.washingtonpost.com/opinions/jesus-doesnt-tweet/2015/04/30/fb07ef1a-ed01-11e4-8666-a1d756d0218e_story.html?noredirect=on&utm_term=.97a37493950d. Last accessed January 9, 2019.

227. Powell, Frank. "10 Reasons Churches Are Not Reaching Millennials." *Frank Powell Online*. June 25, 2014. http://frankpowell.me/ten-reasons-church-absent-millennials/. Last Accessed January 9, 2019.

228. Reiss, Jana. "Why Millennials Are Really Leaving Religion (It's Not Just Politics, Folks)." *Religion News Online: Flunking Sainthood*. June 26, 2018. https://religionnews.com/2018/06/26/why-millennials-are-really-leaving-religion-its-not-just-politics-folks/. Last accessed January 9, 2019.

229. Eaton, S. "12 Reasons Millennials Are Over Church." *Recklessly Alive*. September 29, 2016. http://www.recklesslyalive.com/12-reasons-millennials-are-over-church/. Last accessed January 8, 2019.

230. Morris, G. "Millennials' Reasons for Leaving the Church Don't Hold Up." *Breakpoint Radio Online*. August 31, 2017. http://www.breakpoint.org/2017/08/millennials-reasons-leaving-church-dont-hold/. Last accessed January 14, 2019.

231. Morris, G. "Millennials' Reasons for Leaving the Church Don't Hold Up." *Breakpoint Radio Online*. August 31, 2017. http://www.breakpoint.org/2017/08/millennials-reasons-leaving-church-dont-hold/. Last accessed January 14, 2019.

232. Eaton, S. "12 Reasons Millennials Are Over Church." *Recklessly Alive*. September 29, 2016. http://www.recklesslyalive.com/12-reasons-millennials-are-over-church/. Last accessed January 8, 2019.

233. Eaton, S. "12 Reasons Millennials Are Over Church." *Recklessly Alive*. September 29, 2016. http://www.recklesslyalive.com/12-reasons-millennials-are-over-church/. Last accessed January 8, 2019.

234. Eaton, S. "12 Reasons Millennials Are Over Church." *Recklessly Alive*. September 29, 2016. http://www.recklesslyalive.com/12-reasons-millennials-are-over-church/. Last accessed January 8, 2019.

235. Powell, Frank. "10 Reasons Churches Are not Reaching Millennials." *Frank Powell Online*. June 25, 2014. http://frankpowell.me/ten-reasons-church-absent-millennials/. Last Accessed January 9, 2019.

236. Flory, Nancy. "How Does the Church Reach Millennials? Hint: It's Not Flashing Lights or Rock Band Worship." *The Stream*. October 23, 2016. https://stream.org/how-does-the-church-reach-millennials-hint-its-not-flashing-lights-and-rock-band-worship/. Last accessed January 9, 2019.

237. Flory, Nancy. "How Does the Church Reach Millennials? Hint: It's Not Flashing Lights or Rock Band Worship." *The Stream*. October 23, 2016. https://stream.org/how-does-the-church-reach-millennials-hint-its-not-flashing-lights-and-rock-band-worship/. Last accessed January 9, 2019.

238. "Bio: Keith Green." *Last Days Ministries Online*. https://www.lastdaysministries.org/Groups/1000008700/Last_Days_Ministries/Keith_Green/Bio/Bio.aspx. Last accessed January 15, 2019.

239. "Bio: Keith Green." *Last Days Ministries Online*. https://www.lastdaysministries.org/Groups/1000008700/Last_Days_Ministries/Keith_Green/Bio/Bio.aspx. Last accessed January 15, 2019.

240. Carey, Jesse. "11 Keith Green Songs That Changed Worship Music: A Look at His Legacy 33 Years after His Tragic Death." *Relevant Magazine Online*. July 28, 2015. https://relevantmagazine.com/culture/11-keith-green-songs-helped-change-worship-music. Last accessed January 15, 2019.

241. "Bio: Keith Green." *Last Days Ministries Online*. https://www.lastdaysministries.org/Groups/1000008700/Last_Days_Ministries/Keith_Green/Bio/Bio.aspx. Last accessed January 15, 2019.

242. "Bio: Keith Green." *Last Days Ministries Online*. https://www. lastdaysministries.org/Groups/1000008700/Last_Days_Ministries/ Keith_Green/Bio/Bio.aspx. Last accessed January 15, 2019.

243. "Bio: Keith Green." *Last Days Ministries Online*. https://www. lastdaysministries.org/Groups/1000008700/Last_Days_Ministries/ Keith_Green/Bio/Bio.aspx. Last accessed January 15, 2019.

244. "Bio: Keith Green." *Last Days Ministries Online*. https://www. lastdaysministries.org/Groups/1000008700/Last_Days_Ministries/ Keith_Green/Bio/Bio.aspx. Last accessed January 15, 2019.

245. "Bio: Keith Green." *Last Days Ministries Online*. https://www. lastdaysministries.org/Groups/1000008700/Last_Days_Ministries/ Keith_Green/Bio/Bio.aspx. Last accessed January 15, 2019.

246. "Bio: Keith Green." *Last Days Ministries Online*. https://www. lastdaysministries.org/Groups/1000008700/Last_Days_Ministries/ Keith_Green/Bio/Bio.aspx. Last accessed January 15, 2019.

247. Green, Keith. *The Ministry Years: Volume 1; 1977–1979: "My Eyes Are Dry."* Chatsworth, CA: Sparrow, 1988. Pp. 159–160.

248. Green, Keith. *The Ministry Years: Volume 1; 1977–1979: "Asleep In The Light."* Chatsworth, CA: Sparrow, 1988. Pp. 113–115.

249. "Bio: Keith Green." *Last Days Ministries Online*. https://www. lastdaysministries.org/Groups/1000008700/Last_Days_Ministries/ Keith_Green/Bio/Bio.aspx. Last accessed January 15, 2019.

250. Flory, Nancy. "How Does the Church Reach Millennials? Hint: It's Not Flashing Lights or Rock Band Worship." *The Stream Online*. October 23, 2016. https://stream.org/how-does-the-church-reach- millennials-hint-its-not-flashing-lights-and-rock-band-worship/. Last accessed January 15, 2019.

251. Earls, Aaron. "7 Ways to Draw Millennials too Your Church." *Facts & Trends Online*. May 20, 2014. https://factsandtrends. net/2014/05/20/7-ways-to-draw-millennials-to-your-church/. Last accessed January 9, 2019.

252. Earls, Aaron. "7 Ways to Draw Millennials to Your Church."

Facts & Trends Online. May 20, 2014. https://factsandtrends. net/2014/05/20/7-ways-to-draw-millennials-to-your-church/. Last accessed January 9, 2019.

253. Folmsbee, Chris. "Church Leaders Frustrated with Millennial Staff." *Think Burlap.* http://www.thinkburlap.com/blog/ ctf3b6am9j5naptaprae9r4jxy387w. Last accessed January 15, 2019.

254. Cooke, Phil, dir. *Run Baby Run.* United States: Vision Video Inc., 1998. DVD. 52 Minutes. Timestamp 26:50.

255. Wilkerson, David with Sherrill, John and Elizabeth. 1963. *The Cross and the Switchblade.* USA, published for Teen Challenge by Pyramid Publications by arrangement with Bernard Geis Associates. P. 62–63.

256. Wilkerson, David with Sherrill, John and Elizabeth. 1963. *The Cross and the Switchblade.* USA, published for Teen Challenge by Pyramid Publications by arrangement with Bernard Geis Associates. P.63.

257. Cooke, Phil dir. *Run Baby Run.* United States: Vision Video Inc., 1998. DVD. 52 Minutes. Timestamp 28:36–28:56.

258. Cooke, Phil dir. *Run Baby Run.* United States: Vision Video Inc., 1998. DVD. 52 Minutes. Timestamp 28:00–32:00.

259. Wilkerson, David with Sherrill, John and Elizabeth. 1963. *The Cross and the Switchblade.* USA, published for Teen Challenge by Pyramid Publications by arrangement with Bernard Geis Associates. P. 29.

260. Meadows, Caitlyn. "What Millennials Want the Church to Know." *Artios Magazine Online.* June 12, 2017. https://artiosmagazine.org/ culture/millennials-want-church-know/. Last Accessed January 9, 2019.

261. Meadows, Caitlyn. "What Millennials Want the Church to Know." *Artios Magazine Online.* June 12, 2017. https://artiosmagazine.org/ culture/millennials-want-church-know/. Last Accessed January 9, 2019.

262. Skeldon, Grant. "Millennials Answer, 'Why Are Millennials Leaving the Church?'" March 27, 2018. YouTube Video, 5:55. https://www.youtube. com/watch?v=QhsQrQ2y4NM. Last accessed January 11, 2019.

263. C.S. Lewis> Quotes> Quotable Quote. "If we find ourselves with

a desire that nothing in this world can satisfy, the most probably explanation is that we were made for another world." https://www. goodreads.com/quotes/6439-if-we-find-ourselves-with-a-desire-that-nothing-in. Last accessed January 16, 2019.

264. C.S. Lewis> Quotes> Quotable Quote. "If you think of this world as a place simply intended for our happiness, you find it quite intolerable: think of it as a place for training and correction and it's not so bad." https://www.goodreads.com/quotes/379881-if-you-think-of-this-world-as-a-place-simply. Last Accessed January 16, 2019.

265. Rimmer, Jordan. "The Millennial's Guide to the Older Generations." *Pittsburg Theological Seminary Online. March* 3, 2015. https://www/ pts.edu/blog/millennials-guide-to-old-people-church/. Last accessed January 16, 2019.

266. Osborn Tramain, "1976 Toyota Corolla Commercial—'You Asked for It, You Got It.'" Youtube Video, :32, January 5, 2016, https://www. youtube.com/watch?v=jVHg1CjqLk8. Accessed November 30, 2018.

267. "Hodiernal." *Oxford Dictionary Online.* https://en.oxforddictionaries. com/definition/hodiernal. Last accessed January 16, 2019.

268. "Hodiernal." *Oxford Dictionary Online.* https://en.oxforddictionaries. com/definition/hodiernal. Last accessed January 16, 2019.

269. The Veritas Forum. "Is Tolerance Intolerant? Pursuing the Climate of Acceptance and Inclusion." February 17, 2013. YouTube Video, 1:46:43. https://www.youtube.com/watch?v=uyTa5r4GG4M. Accessed December 11, 2018.

270. The Veritas Forum. "Is Tolerance Intolerant? Pursuing the Climate of Acceptance and Inclusion." February 17, 2013. YouTube Video, 1:46:43. https://www.youtube.com/watch?v=uyTa5r4GG4M. Accessed December 11, 2018.

271. The Veritas Forum. "Is Tolerance Intolerant? Pursuing the Climate of Acceptance and Inclusion." February 17, 2013. YouTube Video, 1:46:43. https://www.youtube.com/watch?v=uyTa5r4GG4M. Accessed December 11, 2018.

272. Rimmer, Jordan. "The Millennial's Guide to the Older Generations." *Pittsburg Theological Seminary Online. March* 3, 2015. https://www/pts.edu/blog/millennials-guide-to-old-people-church/. Last accessed January 16, 2019.

273. Rimmer, Jordan. "The Millennial's Guide to the Older Generations." *Pittsburg Theological Seminary Online. March* 3, 2015. https://www/pts.edu/blog/millennials-guide-to-old-people-church/. Last accessed January 16, 2019.

274. Earls, Aaron. "7 Ways to Draw Millennials to Your Church." *Facts & Trends Online.* May 20, 2014. https://factsandtrends.net/2014/05/20/7-ways-to-draw-millennials-to-your-church/. Last accessed January 9, 2019.

275. Rishmawy, Derek. "The Church Failed Millennials, Just Not in the Way You Think It Did." *Patheos Online.* July 31, 2013. http://www.patheos.com/blogs/christandpopculture/2013/07/a-plea-to-my-fellow-millennials-about-leaving-the-church/. Last accessed January 16, 2019.

276. Rishmawy, Derek. "The Church Failed Millennials, Just Not in the Way You Think It Did." *Patheos Online.* July 31, 2013. http://www.patheos.com/blogs/christandpopculture/2013/07/a-plea-to-my-fellow-millennials-about-leaving-the-church/. Last accessed January 16, 2019.

277. Rishmawy, Derek. "The Church Failed Millennials, Just Not in the Way You Think It Did." *Patheos Online.* July 31, 2013. http://www.patheos.com/blogs/christandpopculture/2013/07/a-plea-to-my-fellow-millennials-about-leaving-the-church/. Last accessed January 16, 2019.